THE SIXTIES

A Fresh Look at the Decade of Change by Francis Wheen

Century Publishing, London, in association with Channel Four Television Company Limited

THE SIXTIES

Text Copyright © Francis Wheen, 1982
All rights reserved

First published in Great Britain in 1982
by Century Publishing Co. Ltd,
76 Old Compton Street,
London W1V 5PA

British Library Cataloguing in
Publication Data

Wheen, Francis
   The sixties.
   1. Great Britain — Social life and
   customs — 20th century
   I. Title
   941.085′6   DA592
   ISBN 0 7126 0018 3
   ISBN 0 7126 0014 0 Pbk

Text set by Rowland Phototypesetting,
Bury St Edmunds, Suffolk
Printed in Great Britain by
The Thetford Press Ltd, Thetford,
Norfolk

*Book design by
Pearce Marchbank.
Photo research by
Susan Ready.*
*Artwork by Perry Neville and
Sue Tritton.*
*All photographs from John
Topham Picture Library
(except where otherwise stated).*
*Cover designed by Pearce Marchbank
and photographed by Gered
Mankowitz.*
*Properties courtesy of Sue Ready,
Miles, Heather Page, Richard Evans,
Ronnie Melia of Radar, The Ephemera
Society, Don Atyeo, John Frost, Pearce
Marchbank, Tariq Ali, Ben Sutton, The
Labour Party, Phil Levene.*

I am grateful to all the
journalists and authors whose
work on particular aspects of
the 1960s provided useful raw
material. I have appended a
select bibliography listing
publications which I found
particularly stimulating.
   The appearance of this book
owes much to the efforts of
Gail Rebuck, Sarah Wallace,
Pearce Marchbank, Sue Ready,
Pat Kavanagh and Michael
Jackson. Thanks are also due
to Kate Walker, Martin
Walker, Julia Watson, Frankie
Cole, Sarah Benton, Patrick
Wintour, Peter Kellner, Gillian
Wilce, Christopher Hird,
Christopher Hitchens, Susan
Campbell, Sue Roles, Tariq
Ali, Jane Thomas, Nicholas de
Jongh, John Coleman, Perry
Neville, Sue Tritton, Frank
Wally and Alan Smith at John
Topham Photo Library. To my
parents I owe more gratitude
than I can express.
Francis Wheen

The Sixties is an RSO production for
Channel Four.
Executive Producer, Graham Benson
Series Producer, Michael Jackson
Producer/Director, David Pearson

27½ YARDS OF RIBBON AND 154 METAL FASTENERS — "UNDERWEAR AN OPTIONAL EXTRA" CHELSEA FASHION SHOW, SEPTEMBER 1967

YOUTH

Teddy boys and the birth of youth culture . . . arrival of rock'n'roll . . . angry young men . . . record companies discover the teenage market . . . Tommy Steele . . . teenage gangs set up their own rock'n'roll groups . . . Mersey Beat comes to town . . . Beatles praised by politicians, press and royalty . . . the Fab Four conquer

America . . . ghost of the teds returns in the shape of mods and rockers . . . mods' early interest in modern jazz and rhythm'n'blues . . . devotion to dressing well . . . dancing and pill-popping . . . mods called 'sawdust Caesars' after seaside troubles . . . adults worried by unattached youngsters . . . protest about having to bend over backwards to please teenagers

. . . pirate radio forced off the air . . . Mary Quant opens Kings Road boutique . . . John Stephen sets up shop in Carnaby Street . . . tourists and telly crews move in to Carnaby Street, mods move out . . . mini-skirts, Vidal Sassoon, Biba, Twiggy . . . flower power . . . pop goes psychedelic . . . mysteries of the Orient . . . drugs and hippies . . . underground press . . . Lennon and Yoko go to bed . . . alternative society and counter-culture . . . cult of ska and reggae . . . skinheads beat up hippies . . . rock singers become tycoons . . . **page 14**

POLITICS

'Never had it so good' . . . Harold Macmillan and the aristocrats . . . Harold Wilson and the scientists . . . Profumo scandal . . . Wilson comes to Downing Street . . . the pound takes a battering . . . Wilson compared to Duke of Wellington, Walter Mitty, John F. Kennedy, Yorkshire terrier . . . Morecambe and Wise invited to

Downing Street . . . Wilson wins World Cup . . . Wilson and Vietnam . . . America calls Wilson new Churchill, China calls him 'a nitwit' . . . immigration laws tightened . . . Enoch Powell still not happy . . . Labour supporters fed up with Wilson . . . collapse of seamen's strike after Wilson's intervention . . . deflation and wage freeze . . . Queen praises trades unions . . . gap between union leaders and members . . . students' revolt . . . sit-in at LSE . . . Paris uprising . . . demo in Grosvenor Square . . . growth of far Left . . . end of the Wilson era . . . **page 54**

SEX

'Casual promiscuity' of late 1950s . . . *Lady Chatterley* put on trial and acquitted . . . upper-class sex antics revealed in 1963 . . . Christine Keeler and Mandy Rice-Davies . . . 'country-house orgies' . . . 'Are we going sex crazy?' . . . television and films start to mention sex . . . Kenneth Tynan's four-letter word . . . Mary Whitehouse attacks 'suggestive and erotic' filth . . . BBC's new chairman offended by 'knickers' . . . Alf Garnett goes off the air . . . sex and theatre censorship . . . Joe Orton's play 'a disgusting piece of filth' . . .

Hair and *Oh! Calcutta!* . . . X certificate films . . . James Bond and his women . . . strip clubs . . . porn magazines . . . sex in underground press . . . *Oz* charged with obscenity . . . Germaine Greer writes *The Female Eunuch* . . . sexual politics for women and gays . . . homosexual laws changed . . . rules on divorce and abortion also reformed . . . teenagers and sex . . . legacy of the permissive society . . . **page 90**

CLASS

Macmillan announces end of class war . . . most aristocratic government in living memory . . . working-class characters begin to appear in plays and films . . . cult of 'classlessness' in 1960s . . . David Frost, Michael Caine, Twiggy, David Bailey . . . upper-class figures such as Lord Snowdon attracted by working-class vitality . . . public schoolboys buy Beatles records . . . some lower-middle-class people able to rise in social status through

grammar schools and universities . . . Harold Wilson and Ted Heath . . . other people condemned to 'life sentence' in working class . . . manual workers become more affluent . . . middle-class backlash . . . 'live now, pay later' destroys middle-class habit of thrift . . . highest positions in Britain still occupied by people from public schools . . . John Lennon and Albert Finney on class divisions . . . **page 114**

MONEY

Popularity of gambling in 1960s . . . ideal of 'quick money, quick fame' . . . old Establishment fascinated by new tycoons . . . Kray brothers and Richardsons . . . great train robbers

become folk heroes . . . David Frost, the man who 'rose without trace' . . . Frost becomes millionaire and TV franchise-holder . . . television companies' 'licence to print money' . . . the rise and fall of Slater Walker . . . Slater's money-making techniques . . . fortunes made by property developers . . . Harry Hyams and Centre Point . . . the Rachman affair . . . Emil Savundra's insurance fraud . . . new tycoons lose their glamour . . . **page 132**

WORK &PLAY

Automation and the changing nature of work . . . boom in 'service industry' . . . 'I'm Backing Britain' campaign . . . shorter working hours . . . influence of work on leisure . . . sport, entertainment, tourism . . . offices become more like homes . . . Richard Neville and the dream of 'play power' . . . communes . . . new housing estates break up old communities . . . supermarkets and shopping centres . . . popularity of television hurts cinema and sports . . . British families become motorised . . . pubs go upmarket . . . package holidays in Spain . . . new interest in foreign food . . . Habitat, stripped pine and 'conspicuous thrift' . . . peasant *chic* . . . consumer campaigns for real bread and real ale . . . still no real television . . . **page 152**

The 1960s were different. It may be a cliché but it's worth repeating because, as Britain limps towards the mid-1980s, there is a new generation which did not live through the 1960s and is understandably sceptical of the claims its elders make for that notorious decade. But it was not as different as some people would have us believe. In the 1960s the success of Michael Caine or Ted Heath was interpreted as evidence that Britain was fast becoming a 'classless society'. Yet when Margaret

YOUNG UNEMPLOYED LOBBY PARLIAMENT, FEBRUARY 1964

Thatcher formed her Cabinet in 1979 it contained just two people who had not been educated at public schools—exactly the same number as in Alec Douglas-Home's Cabinet of 1963.

Does this mean that the undoubted excitement of the 1960s was mere sound and fury, signifying nothing? I think not, although there is plenty of evidence one could use to support the claim. Stars of all kinds shone with a brilliant intensity and then,

as often as not, swiftly burned themselves out. No wonder Andy Warhol came up with his famous line that in future everyone would be famous for fifteen minutes.

However, although many of the people and fashions that enjoyed such fame in the 1960s did not last much longer than Warhol's statutory quarter of an hour, some of the changes in attitude which they promoted have proved rather more durable. The revolutionary break in high culture which occurred in the 1920s

MILLIONTH MINI COMES OFF THE LINE DRIVEN BY DESIGNER ALEC ISSIGONIS. FEBRUARY 1965

(through such artists as Le Corbusier, Pound, Eliot, Stravinsky and Joyce) was paralleled by the break in popular culture and lifestyles which took place in the 1960s. In both cases there was a reaction against them—one thinks of Mary Whitehouse's protests, the skinheads' disenchantment with rock music, and, most recently, Margaret Thatcher's claim that the 1960s had weakened the nation's moral fibre. Yet in neither case was it possible simply to revert to the status quo

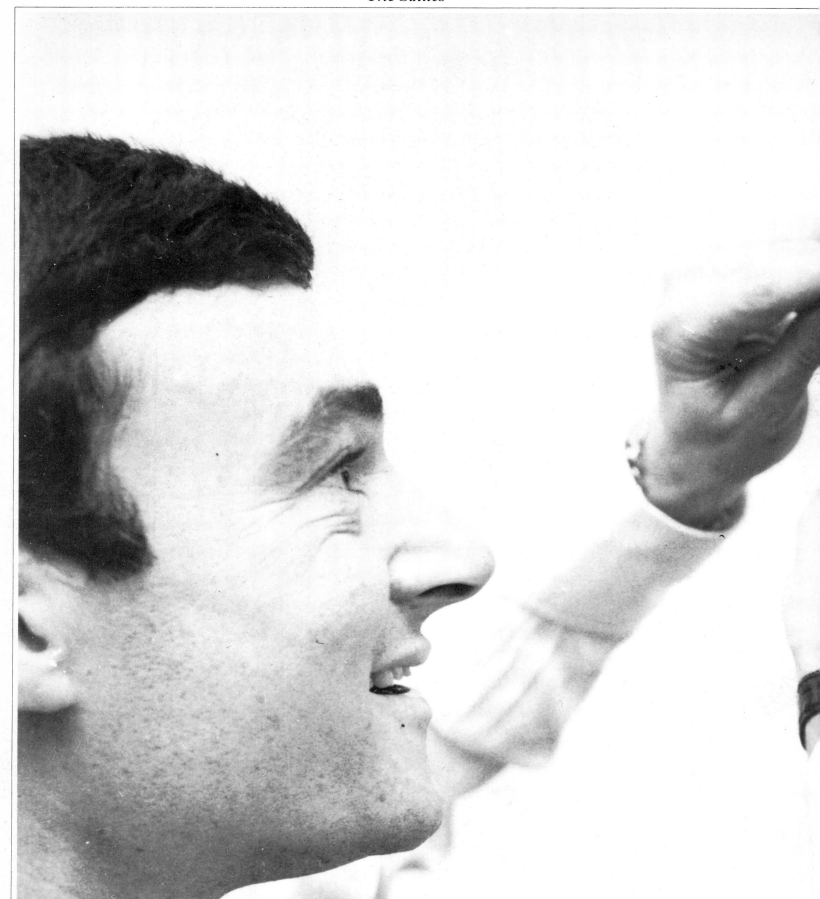

ante. An artist in the 1980s who dislikes Picasso is nevertheless unable to behave as though he never existed. The same goes for the innovations of the 1960s: the whole language has been altered.

Roy Jenkins once said that 'the permissive society is the civilised society'. Those who disagreed with him pointed to the disagreeable side effects of permissiveness, such as strip clubs or advertisements which used scantily clad women. Yet Jenkins

VIDAL SASSOON GIVES MARY QUANT A TRIM (PHOTO: SYNDICATION INTERNATIONAL)

was right. In the 1960s Britain became a much more civilised country in which to live, even though it was, obviously, far from perfect. Prison conditions remained a national scandal, but the death penalty was abolished. Homosexual activity was legalised only for consenting adults over the age of twenty-one, but gay people became more confident in openly admitting their sexuality.

If I sometimes seem to be adopting a critical tone in the pages that follow, it is

not because I wish to suggest that the 1960s promised much and delivered nothing but because I believe a corrective is needed to the rose-coloured memories which distance can easily create. It has become common to speak of the 'revolution' of the 1960s as if it were a neatly unified whole. In fact, the decade was a higgledy-piggledy collection of revolutions which were going on simultaneously. Some were successful; others left a scar. In order to distinguish these revolutions I have

TOM JONES, ENGLEBERT HUMPERDINCK AND THEIR MANAGER, FEBRUARY 1969

divided the book into chapters on different themes rather than attempting a chronological approach.

Now that the decade has been in its grave for a number of years, a fresh assessment is possible—examining not only the ways in which the Sixties differed from its predecessors, but also the way in which it continues to affect our lives today.

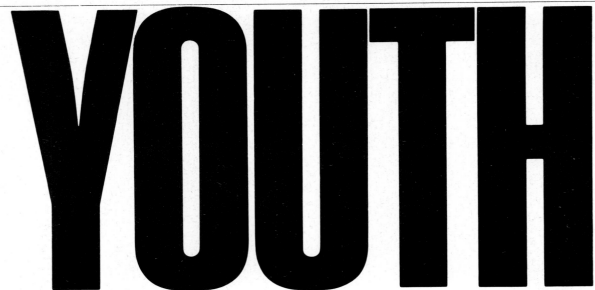

YOUTH

'Our generation had to find something else' Pete Townshend.
'I had always wanted young people to have a fashion of their own, absolutely Twentieth Century fashion' Mary Quant.

One of the most enduring memories of the 1960s is that of the 'youth revolution', a hold-all containing everyone from Twiggy to Tariq Ali, from the mods to the hippies. Did these people have anything in common other than the fact that they all happened to be young? It is time to empty the hold-all and examine its contents.

There is a prevalent belief that the start of the youth revolution coincided with the economic boom of the late Fifties and early Sixties—the time when, according to Harold Macmillan, many people had 'never had it so good'. In fact the earliest manifestation of a distinctive youth culture anticipated the Macmillan era by several years. In 1950, while Britain was still going through its obligatory period of post-war austerity, a group of Savile Row tailors introduced a new version of the Edwardian suit; its main elements were narrow trousers, fancy waistcoats and long jackets with narrow lapels. After years in which men's clothes had been notable for their drabness the tailors were attempting to re-create the style of an earlier age, and they intended their suits to be worn by smart young gentlemen about town. The new look enjoyed only a modest success among the aristocratic youths of Mayfair, but it was taken up by a quite different set of people—'spivs' and other shady characters in the working-class districts of South London. Youths in the same areas began to imitate them. The teddy boy was born.

The earliest teddy boys came from the poorest section of the working class. They lived in some of the most squalid housing in Britain. They had been failures at school (quite a few of them were illiterate). Although they were better off than their counterparts a generation before, they were still far from affluent; in many cases, the only way in which they could obtain the money for their Edwardian suits was by stealing. Even if the much-heralded economic boom did take place, they could not see that it would be of much benefit to them: they would still be working at the same dead-end jobs. A comment made by Pete Townshend of The Who in 1965, although it referred to the mods, applied equally to the teddy boys: 'Two wars gave youngsters something to identify with. Our generation had to find something else.' The first teds found it by expropriating the dress of upper-class dandies and then making it their own, adding refinements such as moleskin or velvet lapels, drainpipe trousers, suede shoes and bootlace ties.

The teddy boys' outfit had several functions. One was to cock a snook at people who were better off: even if the teds would never have the money and opportunities of the rich, they could at least dress like them. It was a gesture of subversion, and it was recognised as such: by 1954 there were reports of Bertie Wooster types hurriedly emptying their wardrobes of Edwardian suits, unable to bear the pejorative associations which their clothes had acquired. Another motive behind the teds' adoption of this style was to find something in which they could take pride. Their jobs or homes would never fulfil this need, but the 'teddy boy look' did so perfectly. Teds therefore became extremely touchy about any insult, however slight, to their appearance. The first 'teddy boy murder' took place on Clapham Common in 1953 after a ted had been called a 'flash cunt' by another youth who wasn't a ted. This killing marked the point at which newspapers began to depict teds as a public enemy.

Such a description of themselves didn't worry the teds at all. It gave them a status in society and, as far as they were concerned, any status was better than none. One of the main functions of the teds' style of dress was that it gave them a sense of belonging to a group. There had been youth movements before, of course, and some of them had had their own uniforms, but all of them—whether the Girl Guides or the Hitler Youth—had been organised and controlled from above, by adults in the ruling class. The teddy boys were the first identifiable dissident youth movement, independent both of the adults in their own class and of young people in other classes. The uniform was a symbol of their group identity, and in this they set a trend that was to be followed by mods, rockers, rude boys and skinheads among others.

Within a couple of years the teddy-boy cult had spread far beyond the London slum areas, taken up by young people not nearly as badly off as the original teds. When rock'n'roll crossed the Atlantic, teds took to it instantly. In 1956 Bill Haley's film *Rock Around the Clock* came to Britain and caused riots wherever it was shown, with teenagers tearing out seats and attacking cinema staff. Public reaction to these events was typified by the clergyman who declared in a sermon that 'rock'n'roll is a revival of devil-dancing', adding that it would 'turn young people into devil-worshippers' and 'provoke lawlessness'. Newspapers began to use the term 'teddy boy' to abuse anyone who seemed to threaten the established order; John Osborne was described as 'an intellectual teddy boy' when his play *Look Back in Anger* was staged in 1956.

The real explanation for the violence of teddy boys between 1955 and 1958 had nothing to do with devil worship. By the mid-1950s many affluent youths had joined the teds. They listened to Bill Haley; and from May 1956 onwards, when Elvis Presley entered the British charts with both 'Heartbreak Hotel' and 'Blue Suede Shoes', they listened to an even more authentic expression of teenage energy. They watched the youthful assertiveness of Marlon Brando in *The Wild Ones* or James Dean in *Rebel Without a Cause*. But when they left the cinema, or turned off the gramophone, there was nowhere for them to go. In most British towns social life centred round the dance hall, which catered for people in their twenties or thirties who had 'settled down' to family life, or the pub. Most teds were under the legal drinking age

anyway, but even those who were allowed into pubs didn't feel much excitement at the thought of spending their evening watching old men playing shove ha'penny or darts. The alternatives were to stand on street corners or sit in dreary cafés. It was hardly surprising that their frustration sometimes erupted into violence.

Some cafés took the hint and installed juke-boxes. This mollified the teds slightly, but it was hardly a satisfactory solution; for one thing, it was impossible to dance in cafés. Richard Hoggart described a typical café or 'milk bar' in his book *The Uses of Literacy*, published in 1957:

> The records seem to be changed about once a fortnight by the hiring firm; almost all are American; almost all are 'vocals' and the styles of singing much advanced beyond what is normally heard on the Light Programme of the BBC . . . The 'nickelo-deon' is allowed to blare out so that the noise would be sufficient to fill a good-sized ballroom, rather than a converted shop in the main street. The young men waggle one shoulder or stare, as desperately as Humphrey Bogart, across the tubular chairs.

While the teds sat disconsolately in their milk bars, another group of young people were staging a small revolt. In May 1956 the Royal Court Theatre in London put on John Osborne's play *Look Back in Anger*. The play's hero, Jimmy Porter, was a young working-class man who mocked the 'chinless wonders' of the upper classes, even though he himself was married to an upper-class girl called Alison. One or two papers found the play offensive, but most of the liberal intelligentsia—the very people whom Osborne was supposed to be attacking—loved it. The phrase 'angry young men' was invented as a generic title for a number of lower-middle-class writers of the period. Apart from Osborne, they included Kingsley Amis, whose novel *Lucky Jim* had been published in 1954; John Braine, the author of *Room at the Top*, published in 1957; and Colin Wilson, whose philosophical treatise, *The Outsider*, appeared in 1956.

The reaction to the angry young men is instructive, for it was to be repeated several times in the 1960s. The ruling order was confronted with a challenge. Instead of clamping down straight away, it first tried to defuse it by 'buying off' the leaders—praising them, rewarding them and flattering them into acquiescence. The Establishment could thereby 'prove' that it was not a collection of fuddy-duddies after all. This process was visible in many areas during the 1960s—as when, for example, the master of Brasenose College, Oxford, invited the Beatles to dinner—and it was also discernible in the hyperbole used to acclaim the angry young men. The results were impressive: by the 1980s Kingsley Amis, John Braine and John Osborne were content to be thought of as crusty old reactionaries, fulminating against anything vaguely 'progress-ive' in politics or the arts.

Youthful rebellion was also defused by the commercial in-terests—record companies, clothes shops, the media—who, by the late 1950s, had discovered the existence of a lucrative teenage market. It would be foolish to claim, as some have done, that the youth sub-cultures from the 1950s to the 1980s were actually created by these forces: there is no doubt that the teddy boys, the mods and the punk-rockers arose, unprompted, from the teen-agers themselves. What commerce did was to take one of these spontaneous movements and cash in on it, while simultaneously

Age of the coffee bar: 'The records seem to be changed about once a fortnight by the hiring firm...the styles of singing much advanced beyond what is normally heard on the Third Programme on the BBC.... The noise would be sufficient to fill a good-sized ballroom'.

COFFEE BAR, 1960

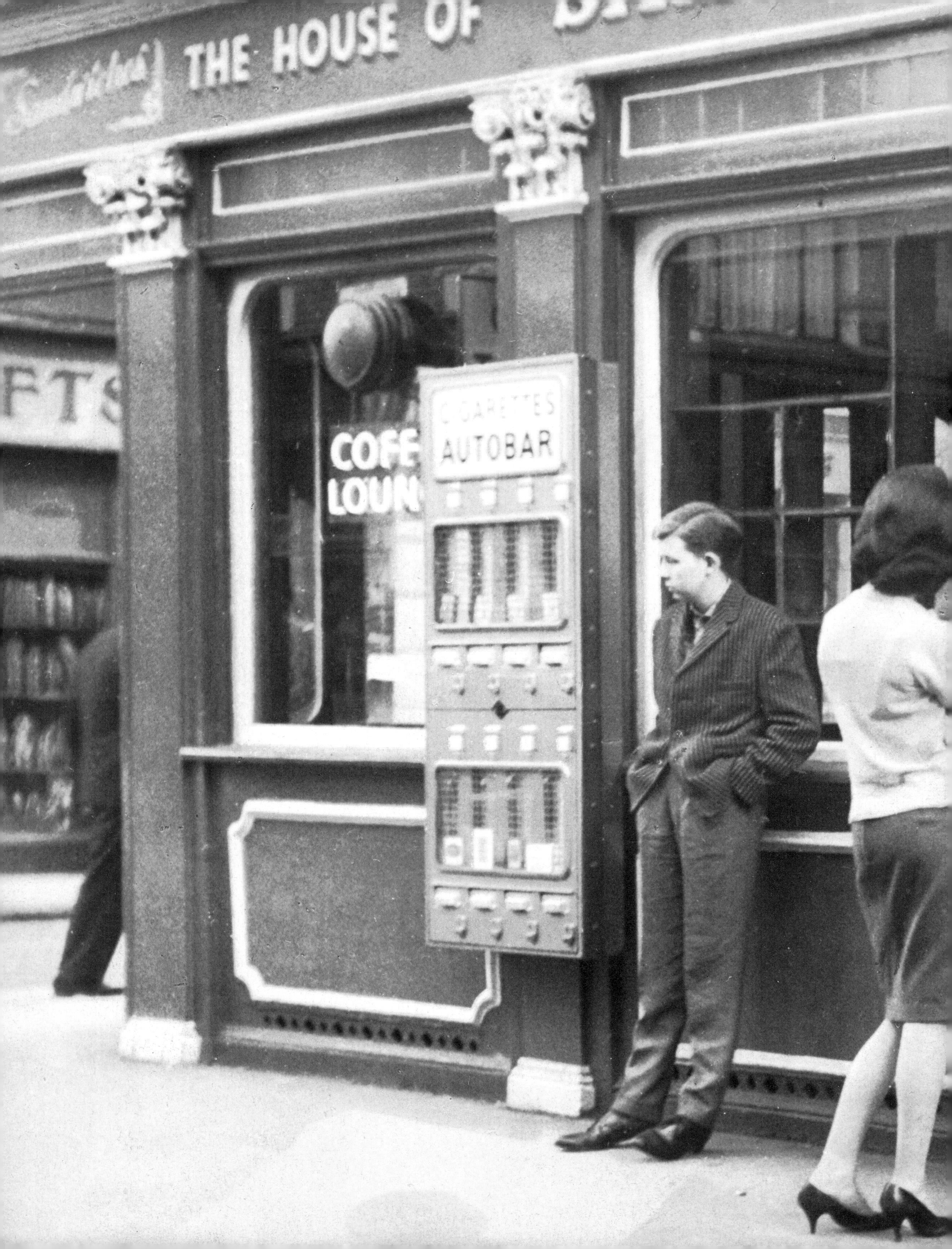
THE HOUSE OF
CIGARETTES
AUTOBAR
COFE
LOUN
FTS

trying to control its direction and so keep it clear of any 'unhealthy' tendencies. One of the most illuminating accounts of this process was given by Sir John Read, chairman of EMI, at his company's 1976 annual general meeting, when he was coming under pressure to cancel the Sex Pistols' recording contract:

> Throughout its history as a recording company, EMI has always sought to behave within contemporary limits of decency and good taste—taking into account not only the traditional rigid conventions of one section of society, but also the increasingly liberal attitudes of other (perhaps larger) sections . . . EMI should not set itself up as a public censor, but it does seek to encourage restraint.

Similar thoughts inspired the launching of Britain's first home-grown rock'n'roller, Tommy Steele. At the start of 1956 he was plain Tommy Hicks, a merchant seaman who played the guitar in coffee bars in his spare time. He was discovered by an extremely astute entrepreneur called John Kennedy, who decided that Tommy could be marketed as 'the British Elvis Presley'. Within months a recording deal had been arranged with Decca, television appearances had been organised and the script was being written for Tommy's first film, *The Tommy Steele Story*. The film was a rags-to-riches account of Tommy Steele's life, and its message was plain enough: any young person with talent and ambition could be a success. It was followed by a film called *The Duke Wore Jeans*, which aimed to show that, despite their wealth and pomp, the aristocracy were just as keen on rock'n'roll as any teddy boy. Tommy Steele had none of the pouting menace of Elvis. He was essentially pure, and even the sober monthly journal *Encounter* was enthusiastic: 'He is Pan, he is Puck, he is every nice young girl's boy, every kid's favourite elder brother, every mother's cherished adolescent son . . . Mums adore him.' The author of the article, Colin MacInnes, later wrote that 'when one pauses to think what the "top English teenage singer" of the 1950s might have turned out to be . . . one can be grateful that fate . . . gave us so honest and healthy a young man as Tommy Steele.'

The success of Britain's first rock'n'roller signalled the effective end of the teddy boys. Many of them found his music tame by comparison with the American singers such as Elvis or Little Richard, but the idea of instant fame and wealth—constantly stressed in Tommy's publicity—was an alluring dream. Moreover it had not escaped the teds' notice that girls were greatly attracted to rock'n'roll singers who had 'made it'. Many members of teenage gangs lost interest in fighting and devoted their time instead to mastering a few guitar chords.

Colin Fletcher was in one of the numerous gangs on Merseyside at the time. He later wrote an article for the magazine *New Society* describing the effects of the emergence of British rock'n'roll. All over Merseyside gangs gave birth to rock groups, and the group became the gang's new totem: 'What mattered now was not how many boys a gang could muster for a Friday night fight but how well their group played on Saturday night.' Gang members pooled their money to enable 'their' group to buy amplifiers and instruments. Girls, whose role had previously been peripheral, were brought in as seamstresses to make the stage uniforms. Meanwhile the gangs lost their more violent members, who felt that the gang's function was being undermined. And, in time, the gangs lost the groups themselves, who were soon performing every night. Instead, the gangs became 'an organisational centre for going to dances'. With this development the girls became even more important, since they were required as dancing partners. Beat clubs were opened, including a dark, sweaty basement in Liverpool which was christened The Cavern.

One of the 300 beat groups formed in Liverpool in 1960 was the

Teddy boys: Clergymen reviled them as 'devil worshippers' and the press considered them public enemy number one, yet they made possible the success of Tommy Steele, a wholesome rock'n'roller who was 'every kid's favourite elder brother, every mother's cherished son'.

TEDS AT THE MECCA DANCE HALL, TOTTENHAM, LONDON IN THE 1950s (PHOTO: BBC HULTON PICTURE LIBRARY)

Silver Beatles. They played regularly at the Cavern Club, and soon began to make frequent appearances further afield, at the Star Club in Hamburg. It was during their stay there that they adopted a new hairstyle, later to be known as the 'Beatle mop'. Despite lobbying by their manager, Brian Epstein, no fewer than five large record companies turned down the chance of offering the Beatles a recording contract, and it was not until May 1962 that another company, Parlophone, agreed to take them on. A month before their first recording session the Beatles sacked their drummer, Pete Best, and replaced him with Ringo Starr, a member of Rory Storme's Hurricanes. Their first single, 'Love Me Do', was released in October 1962. After getting nowhere for two months it made a brief appearance in the hit parade, reaching No. 17 in the Top 20 before disappearing again.

From then on, however, events moved fast. In February 1963 their next song, 'Please Please Me', reached No. 2 in the chart; by May they had their first No. 1 hit, 'From Me To You'. Their first LP also went to No. 1. On 31 August 1963 the song 'She Loves You' entered the Top 20 and stayed there for an astonishing 24 weeks. Before the year was out it had been followed by yet another No. 1, 'I Want to Hold Your Hand'.

Despite their haircuts the Beatles were clean, pure young lads who were not seen as a threat by the Establishment. They were acceptable to teenagers and their parents, to the popular press and intellectuals, to Tories and socialists. The Conservative prime minister Harold Macmillan praised them as 'our best export'. Following their appearance at the Royal Variety Performance in November 1963 the *Daily Mirror* wrote in its editorial that 'you have to be a real sour square not to love the nutty, noisy, happy, handsome Beatles'. Not to be outdone, the *Sunday Times* called Lennon and McCartney 'the greatest composers since Beethoven', while the classical music critic of *The Times*, William Mann, went into raptures over their 'pandiatonic clusters' and 'flat sub-mediant key switches'. Lennon gave his reaction to William Mann's comments in an interview with *Rolling Stone* some years later: 'He wrote about aeolian cadences and all sorts of musical terms, and he is a bullshitter. But he made us credible with intellectuals . . . it did us a lot of good.' Parents took their children to see the film of *A Hard Day's Night* in 1964; how many did the same for the Sex Pistols' film, *The Great Rock'n'Roll Swindle*, in the 1970s?

The Beatles resembled Tommy Steele both in the speed of their success—from obscurity to Royal Variety Performance in one year—and in their ability to appeal equally to mums and teenagers. Like Steele, they benefited from shrewd 'packaging' by promoters: as Lennon put it later, 'the edges were knocked off. Brian [Epstein] put us in suits and all that and we made it very, very big.'

But there the resemblance ends. Whereas Tommy Steele's music had been bland and unmemorable, the Beatles were genuine innovators. It wasn't simply that they used unusual instruments, such as the harmonica, or new recording techniques, such as double-tracking; having had the rough edges of their rock'n'roll days 'knocked off' they still managed to produce songs of excitement and spontaneity while remaining inside the commercial machine.

Teenagers were thrilled by the novelty and the suddenness of it all. Following the Beatles' success there was an explosion of new groups and singers. Every day, it seemed, some bright young hope was being launched. There were the Mersey groups; there were the solo female singers. Performers came in every shape and size—one group, the Honeycombs, broke new ground by having a female drummer—and most teenagers loved them all. The press tried to manufacture divisions—'Tottenham Sound Has Crushed The Beatles' ran the *Daily Express* headline when the Dave Clark Five reached the top of the charts—but as far as most youngsters were concerned there was nothing wrong with enjoying both Dusty

Springfield and the Rolling Stones. This broadness of taste is illustrated by the performers who appeared in the Beatles' Christmas shows in 1964 and 1965. They were, by modern standards, an incongruous assortment: the cheerful inanities of Freddy and the Dreamers; the hip rhythm and blues of the Yardbirds; and the colonial jollity of Rolf Harris, whose first hit had been 'Tie Me Kangaroo Down, Sport'.

On their first visit to the United States, in February 1964, the Beatles' reception was every bit as enthusiastic as at home. 'I Want to Hold Your Hand' had gone to No. 1 in the States the previous month, and it was soon joined by 'She Loves You' and 'Please Please Me'. When they arrived at Kennedy airport the Beatles were greeted by thousands of hysterical fans. Tickets for their concert in Carnegie Hall were changing hands at $100. Their appearances on the nationally screened *Ed Sullivan Show* on television simply confirmed their status.

The Beatles returned from the States to even greater hysteria. To the fans' original adoration had been added a sense of national pride that the four Liverpudlians had conquered the land in which rock'n'roll had originated. It seemed there was nothing the Beatles could not do. In March 1964, a month after the American triumph, John Lennon published a book, *In His Own Write*, which was received with the hyperbole which had by now become obligatory; the *Sunday Times* compared it with the later works of James Joyce. When the film *A Hard Day's Night* was released in July it was granted the Establishment's seal of approval—a royal premiere. This was compounded the following year when the Beatles—all of whom were still in their early twenties—were awarded the MBE. After receiving their medals from the Queen, the Fab Four gave a press conference at which Paul McCartney charmed reporters by calling Buckingham Palace 'a keen pad'. A disgruntled few returned their own MBEs in protest at the honouring of the Beatles, but most people thought the awards were well deserved. Writing in his diary at the end of the decade, Dick Crossman, a Labour Cabinet minister, believed that the government had been quite right to give the Beatles their medals: 'How respectable they seem now, how useful, how neat their hair-cuts and their dark blue suits.'

The Beatles' brand of respectability was not, however, to everyone's liking. While most teenagers joined Prince Philip in enthusing about the mop-tops, a significant minority found the whole business deeply distasteful. The ghost of the teddy boys returned to haunt Britain in a new form—that of the mods and rockers.

The teddy boys had, in fact, never disappeared. They had simply moved on. Many gave themselves over to the new British rock-'n'rollers of the late Fifties and early Sixties, but a few found the music pretty tame by comparison with the American originals. Members of this latter group devoted themselves to modern jazz, dismissing as 'old-fashioned' the trad jazz revival which was being led in Britain by musicians such as Acker Bilk and Kenny Ball. Their heroes were Charlie Mingus and Dave Brubeck, and they styled themselves 'modernists'—which was swiftly abbreviated to 'mods'. By about 1961 they were also taking an interest in other black American artists, particularly rhythm and blues singers such as Ray Charles and Muddy Waters. This sort of music was never played on the radio in Britain, but the mods found that they could pick it up by tuning in to American forces' stations broadcasting from Europe. The records were hard to obtain, but could occasionally be bought through importers; American sailors passing through ports such as Liverpool would sometimes bring records with them. A small and rather secretive network of enthusiasts was built up in various towns. Being in Liverpool, John Lennon was better placed than most to buy records by his black heroes. He later described the cult:

It was black music we dug . . . We felt very exclusive and underground in Liverpool listening to all those old-time records. And nobody was listening to any of them except Eric Burdon in Newcastle and Mick Jagger in London. It was that lonely. It was fantastic.

Some members of the modernist cult maintained the teddy boys' tradition of being meticulous in their dress. However, whereas the

Love me do: 'You have to be a real sour square not to love the nutty, noisy, happy, handsome Beatles,' wrote the Daily Mirror. *Before they had time to catch their breath, the Fab Four found themselves being lionised as 'the greatest composers since Beethoven'.*

teds' style had been ostentatious, the mods' approach was more refined. Their hair was short and neat. The bastardised version of the Edwardian suit was replaced by impeccably cut Italian suits in conservative colours, which were worn with handmade shoes, shirts with pointed collars and knitted ties. The mods acquired an obsessive fastidiousness about even the smallest details of their appearance, and would have long and intense debates about whether the side-vents on their jackets ought to be one inch or two inches long. The style was a private gesture of subversion, which did not have to be put away when the mods were at work or in school: to the outside world they looked like well-dressed young men. But in the mods' view they were actually undermining conventional standards by carrying smartness to such fussy extremes. As one of them put it, 'if you're a mod, you're a mod twenty-four hours a day; even working with other people, you're still a mod.' The mods' deliberately esoteric attitude led them to go to French films and sit in French clubs in London—even though very few of them spoke French—because they believed that French style epitomised all that was cool and 'unyobbish'.

The clothes-consciousness of these early mods spread to other teenagers. Some of them had scooters, and so they took to wearing parkas—long khaki coats—to protect their clothes from the weather. As a consequence, the parka became fashionable in itself. Casual wear for mods also began to develop, with Fred Perry tennis shirts and Levi jeans being thought particularly desirable. The mods invented their own walk, and even their own stance for use when hanging around on street corners (if you were wearing a jacket, you were allowed to keep only one hand in your trouser pocket).

The male mods were so obsessed with clothes that they didn't have much time for girls, but gradually girls too created their own mod style. They used heavy eye make-up but no lipstick. They often wore men's shirts and trousers, with round-toed shoes. While male mods expressed their defiance by taking exaggerated care over their appearance, the female mods did so by wearing clothes which had until then been regarded as unfeminine.

The leaders of mod fashion, known as the 'faces', tended to buy their outfits in the newly opened boutiques of Carnaby Street; and they were prepared to spend astonishing sums of money. They thought nothing of paying over £4 for a shirt. When The Who were launched, their manager, Kit Lambert, boasted that the group spent £150 a week on clothes and devoted three hours every fortnight to having their hair done.

It was a busy life. A mod called Denzil, interviewed in the *Sunday Times* magazine in 1964, described an 'average' week. On Monday night he would go dancing at the Mecca, the Hammersmith Palais, the Purley Orchard or the Streatham Locarno. On Tuesday night he would be at the Scene Club in Soho. Wednesday was Marquee night, while Thursday was set aside for hair-washing. On Friday he would be back at the Scene Club. Saturday afternoon

Soho goes mod: When The Who's manager wanted to launch them as the first 'mod' pop group he took them to Carnaby Street to make sure that they were kitted out in the correct style. But when the tourists and TV crews moved in, the mods moved out.

WHIT MONDAY AT MARGATE, 1964

FOLLOWER OF FASHION IN KINGS ROAD. OVERLEAF: READY, STEADY, GO, 1966

Seaside mods: The Daily Mirror *thought it 'a pity, in a way, we can't just hand over a few old deckchairs and a deserted chunk of Brighton beach and seal it off and let them play their ridiculous kids' games so we could snooze in the sun in peace. But they wouldn't care for that.'*

was spent shopping for clothes and records; after that he would go out dancing and would rarely return before 9 o'clock on Sunday morning. On Sunday evening he would go to the Flamingo or, if he was flagging, he might get an early night.

Obviously only a few mods maintained a schedule as hectic as this, but there is no doubt that many did burn the candle at both ends. They were enabled to do this by frequent consumption of amphetamines with exotic names like purple hearts, French blues and black bombers. In order to keep up the energy required for dancing, many mods spent every evening 'blocked' on purple heart pills, which could be bought for 6d each in mod clubs.

The mod cult went from strength to strength in the early 1960s, but initially it received little outside attention. In 1962 *Town* magazine interviewed several teenage mods and described the kind of clothes they wore. In 1963 the *Hairdressers' Journal* introduced its readership to the new look:

> Modernists, or mods for short, account for about 35 per cent of Britain's male teenage population. Their fashions are the furthest-out, the most up-to-the-second of any, and the male mod probably devotes between a quarter and a third of his weekly income to his appearance. As such, they represent a valuable clientele to the men's hairdresser who is prepared to give them the sleek, carefully-groomed styles they are looking for.

The estimate that mods accounted for 35 per cent of the male teenage population seemed exaggerated, but it may not have been very far out. Early in 1964 at least five magazines which were aimed at the 'mod market' began publication. The weeklies sold about half a million copies each, while the average circulation of the monthlies was a quarter of a million. One of these papers, *Ready,*

Steady, Go, was related to a weekly television programme of the same name which had begun as a general pop music show but was quickly adopted by the mods. It was broadcast at a highly suitable time—just after six o'clock on a Friday evening, when mods were limbering up for a long weekend of dancing, posing and pill-popping. Dancers on the show came from mod temples such as the Scene Club; *Ready, Steady, Go* thus played an important part in transmitting mod culture to the provinces and suburbs, showing teenagers which dances and clothes were fashionable in any particular week. The programme's presenter, Cathy McGowan, rapidly became established as a mod idol.

By the spring of 1964 the British public was vaguely aware of the existence of mods. Rockers, on the other hand, had received no attention at all. This was partly because there were far fewer rockers than mods but also, more importantly, because rockers were youngsters who wore dirty jeans and leather jackets, whose only great interest was motorbikes. They were therefore not such good targets for commercial exploitation. Fashion pages did not print articles on rockers' clothes or haircuts. Even the motorbike industry did not stand to make much money out of the craze, for rockers prided themselves on their mechanical expertise: if they wanted to improve or repair their bikes, they tended to do it themselves. In March 1964 there was nothing to indicate how suddenly the public's lack of interest in the rockers was to change.

By 1964 it had become common practice for mods to visit the seaside on bank holiday weekends. They would play in the amusement arcades, sit in cafés or walk along the beach. There had not been any reports of violence.

The agreed venue for the mods' outing over the Easter holiday in 1964 was Clacton, a small resort on the Essex coast. Easter day was cold and wet—the coldest for eighty years—and few holidaymakers other than the mods bothered to turn up in Clacton, except some rockers who lived nearby. Shops closed early, exasperated at the lack of business. Several cafés refused to serve the mods. Through sheer boredom some teenagers began to scuffle in the streets, while those with scooters and bikes drove noisily along the front. A few youngsters threw stones.

In view of the fact that the seaside battles of 1964 became thought of as tribal fights between mods and rockers, it is worth noting that at this first incident, in Clacton, the hostility was not so much between these two factions as between the local youngsters (who happened to be rockers) and the 'outsiders' (who happened to be mods).

Newspapers' reaction to the events of Clacton set the tone for all press coverage over the succeeding months. On Easter Monday every paper except *The Times* gave Clacton front-page treatment, using headlines such as 'Day of Terror by Scooter Groups'. The *Daily Mirror*'s story was typical: 'The Wild Ones invaded a seaside town yesterday—1,000 fighting, drinking, roaring, rampaging teenagers on scooters and motorcycles.'

The effect of these reports was predictable: having read their newspapers on the Monday morning a number of teenagers who were looking for a fight descended on Clacton. Further violence followed, and on the Tuesday newspapers were able to run even more sensational stories.

The truth about what happened at Clacton was considerably less dramatic than the national press led their readers to believe. According to the local council, the estimated cost of damage over the weekend was about £500. The home secretary, Henry Brooke, normally regarded as being tough in his attitude to delinquency and vandalism, conceded that most accounts of the violence had been greatly exaggerated: 'There was nothing like a riot or gang warfare. Clacton was not sacked.'

Nevertheless, the image of teenage hoodlums had been successfully planted in the public mind, and newspapers predicted that more seaside violence was bound to follow. These warnings were partly self-fulfilling: any genuine trouble-maker reading that there was to be a punch-up at Margate, for example, would obviously make every effort to be there.

The next bank holiday weekend after the trouble at Clacton was Whitsun. Newspaper photographers and large numbers of police took up their positions in the 'key' towns such as Margate, Brighton and Bournemouth. When the teenagers arrived there was already an air of menace, exacerbated by the discovery that guest houses, cafés and pubs were refusing to open their doors to teenagers. By Saturday no disturbances had been reported, but on the Sunday morning the *News of the World* confidently announced on its front page that Margate was likely to be a trouble-spot.

So it proved. On Sunday morning mods started throwing deck chairs. They also picked up litter and hurled it at the rockers who were driving along the front on their motorbikes. A group of mods chased some rockers along the sea wall. Mounted police and dog handlers forced teenagers on the beach to keep moving, in the belief that this would prevent violence. Its actual effect was precisely the opposite: it created an even greater mêlée, and youngsters who were not involved in the violence found themselves pushed towards areas where fights were taking place. Teenagers who refused to move were arrested. One mod had a piece of driftwood in his hand; as he came off the beach he threw it on to a pile of rubbish. According to his version of the story a policeman told him to 'pick that up, laddie'. He did so—and was promptly arrested for carrying an offensive weapon.

The clashes at Margate made front-page headlines, but once again the reaction was out of all proportion to what had actually occurred. Much was made, for instance, of the smashing of deck chairs by mods; yet the deputy publicity manager of Margate later admitted that the number of deck chairs broken was no greater than on an 'ordinary' bank holiday weekend. The scenes at Margate were described in the press as 'riots' and 'raging battles'; yet only 44 youths were charged with an offence, and 37 of these were accused merely of using threatening language or behaviour. One person was charged with assault, which hardly tallies with the picture of a raging battle.

Public opinion about the events at Margate in Whitsun 1964 was conditioned not by what actually happened—since very few accurate accounts of this were given—but by how other people had reacted to what had happened. The single most influential person in shaping this public view was Dr George Simpson, a Margate magistrate who held a special session of his court on Whit Monday to hear the cases of the 44 youths who had been charged. One of the accused was a 22-year-old mod who pleaded guilty to threatening behaviour. Sentencing him to three months in prison, Dr Simpson made a speech which instantly passed into legend. It is worth quoting in full:

It is not likely that the air of this town had ever been polluted by the hordes of hooligans, male and female, such as we have seen this weekend and of whom you are an example.

These long-haired, mentally unstable, petty little hoodlums, these sawdust Caesars who can only find courage like rats, in hunting in packs, came to Margate with the avowed intent of interfering with the life and property of its inhabitants.

Insofar as the law gives us power, this court will not fail to use the prescribed penalties. It will, perhaps, discourage you and others of your kidney who are infected with this vicious virus.

No one knew what a sawdust Caesar was, but it had a splendid ring about it and headline writers made full use of it. Indeed, the creators of epithets had a field day as they vied with each other to find the most striking description of the teenage 'wild ones'. The youth to whom Dr Simpson had addressed his 'sawdust Caesars' oration had been a short-haired mod, but this had not prevented the magistrate from using the words 'long-haired'. The speech had, in other words, referred not to the boy in the dock but to some unseen but sinister mass outside. Newspapers, politicians and members of the public used the Margate events in the same way—as an excuse to air their general fear of youth. *Time* magazine, in its report on the Whitsun disturbances, declared that

Pirate radio: When the BBC wouldn't play what teenagers wanted to hear, young entrepreneurs moored ships off the coast and set up transmitters. Tony Benn wanted to ban it, and in 1966 he got his way. It was replaced by Wonderful Radio One.

LONDON STREET SCENE, JUNE 1968

teenagers had turned 'holiday into holocaust'; elsewhere mods were described as 'wild morons', 'human wolves', 'dumb brutes' and 'vermin'.

The deep-seated insecurity revealed by these insults had been present since the birth of the teddy-boy cult in the early 1950s, and was caused by 'respectable' adults' realisation that the young were no longer under their control. Whether youths behaved well or badly seemed irrelevant (hence the lack of interest in ascertaining whether there really had been 'riots' at Clacton, Margate or any other seaside resort); what mattered was that youngsters no longer considered themselves obliged to do as they were told by those in authority. Open hostility towards the younger generation was not often displayed before 1964, but hints of it had appeared now and again.

One of the most significant clues emerged in 1960, when the National Association of Youth Clubs expressed its 'concern' at the number of young people who were 'unattached to any kind of youth organisation' (in the eyes of the NAYC such movements as the teddy boys did not, of course, count as 'youth organisations' since they were controlled by youngsters themselves and operated outside the official infrastructure). So great was the NAYC's concern that it applied for a government grant in order to conduct a three-year project in which four youth workers were sent to four different towns in England for three years; the workers' brief was to disguise their true identities and live in the towns as though they were 'normal' youths, so that they could 'make contact with unattached young people, to discover their interests and leisure-time activities'.

The results, published in 1965 under the title 'The Unattached', were a marvellous example of what happens all too often when well-meaning people from officialdom try to 'understand' youngsters. A male research worker, aged twenty-two, moved into the south coast town of 'Seagate' (the identities of the towns, like those of the researchers, were camouflaged). During his first few weeks the researcher visited twelve coffee bars, two jazz clubs, two pubs, one dance hall and an amusement arcade in his search for young people. He found that few were prepared to talk to him; many were highly suspicious of his cover story of being a playwright. Then, after weeks of trying, the worker had a lucky break. He succeeded in striking up a conversation with a young man called Bob in a coffee bar. The researcher wrote later that 'this meeting seemed at the time quite momentous, having spent about two hours with somebody who is obviously unattached and who apparently knows several other young people'. But his hopes were short-lived. Bob was put off by the researcher's enthusiasm to 'get to know him', and the hapless researcher saw his chances of meeting those 'several other young people' receding. However, some weeks later he made contact with some more young people, and he excitedly reported his findings to head office. Young people were not particularly inspired by their jobs; a number of them enjoyed going to parties ('the craze for parties is fanatic; the weekend seems simply not complete unless there has been one, or at least an attempt at one'); a few of them possessed motorbikes and the rest travelled by bus.

The researcher then discovered a juicier piece of information. Outside the church opposite his flat there was a display put on by 'a nautical organisation for young girls'. When he asked a teenager why she didn't belong to it, 'she simply laughed as if I was being funny'. He gloomily inferred that some youngsters 'considered it amusing that people should be concerned about young people. They were able to look after themselves well enough.'

This absurd cloak-and-dagger inquiry lasted for three years and cost thousands of pounds. At the end of it, the organisers concluded that most young people failed to spend their leisure time 'in any demonstrably constructive fashion' as well as showing a

Mini-skirts: Mary Quant wore one to Buckingham Palace to collect her OBE and Diana Rigg had one designed for her to wear in The Avengers, *in spite of protests from television cameramen that it would spoil their concentration. A prize was given for 'the smallest dress in the world'.*

lamentable inability to 'postpone immediate pleasure for the sake of future gain'. Youths had a 'craving for adventure', and displayed a 'pronounced hostility' towards adults in authority—parents, teachers, employers and the police.

The hostility felt by these same adults towards youngsters was not mentioned in the report, but it was revealed again and again in the great mods and rockers scare of 1964. On the Saturday after the Whitsun hysteria the *Daily Mirror* carried a long article by its agony aunt, Marje Proops, about a young mod girl whom she had interviewed. Proops wrote:

> It is a pity, in a way, we can't just hand over a few old deckchairs and a deserted chunk of Brighton Beach and seal it off and let them play their ridiculous kids' games so we could snooze in the sun in peace. But they wouldn't care for that.

Many politicians and journalists at the time made similar statements. What particularly irritated them was that the seaside disturbances did not conform to their preconceptions of what form young people's misbehaviour ought to take. For years young hooligans had committed acts of violence in 'rough' working-class areas, but Establishment opinion had not considered this to be much of a threat because it was invisible: the disorder took place within the young criminals' own enclaves, such as the East End of London, and the middle class therefore did not have to trouble itself too much. The view was well put by Lady Bracknell in *The Importance of Being Earnest*: 'Fortunately in England, at any rate, education produces no effect whatsoever. If it did, it would prove a serious danger to the upper classes, and probably lead to acts of violence in Grosvenor Square.'

At the other end of the scale, there were the 'pranks' and 'japes' perpetrated by youngsters of the upper middle class such as the Bullingdon Club at Oxford University, whose members would get roaring drunk on champagne and go 'baying for broken glass'. The antics of these youths were memorably catalogued by Evelyn Waugh in *Decline and Fall*:

> It was a lovely evening. They broke up Mr Austen's grand piano, and stamped Lord Rending's cigars into his carpet, and smashed his china, and tore up Mr Partridge's sheets, and threw the Matisse into his water-jug; Mr Sanders had nothing to break except his windows . . .

Such outbreaks were put down to no more than youthful high spirits; many adults had indulged in similar behaviour when they were young, and they didn't believe that it had done them any harm.

However, the way in which youth manifested itself in 1964 was unfamiliar and disturbing. The mods did not fit the 'lumpen' image of working-class teenage gangs: they were neat and well-dressed. And instead of remaining on their home ground they travelled to 'respectable' towns and mingled with holiday-making families. The mods were coming worryingly close to acting out Lady Bracknell's vision of working-class youngsters milling about in Grosvenor Square—with the added complication that they didn't look like working-class youngsters. It was all very confusing.

Boutiques: Mary Quant thought that young people 'were tired of wearing essentially the same as their mothers' so she opened Britain's first-ever boutique, Bazaar, to sell 'absolutely twentieth century clothes' to the mini-skirt generation. Business boomed in the King's Road.

There were two main ways of dealing with this difficulty. One was to ignore the evidence and pretend that the mods did correspond to the expected stereotypes—hence the many references to them as long-haired and unkempt (which they clearly were not). The other reaction was to accuse them of ingratitude, as in this comment in the *Glasgow Sunday Mail* in May 1964:

> For years now we've been leaning over backwards to accommodate the teenagers. Accepting meekly on the radio and television that it is *their* music which monopolises the air. That in our shops it is *their* fads which will dictate our dress styles . . .

This theory impressively distorted the history of the previous few years and, in doing so, revealed the ambivalence of contemporary attitudes to youth. Between 1945 and 1960 the wages of teenagers rose twice as fast as those of their parents. Moreover, youngsters were not burdened with the same financial obligations as adults—rent, rates, bills, hire purchase payments and so on. Colin MacInnes, one of the few writers who took the trouble to observe teenagers in the 1950s, declared in 1958 that 'we are in the presence of an entirely new phenomenon in human history: that youth is rich'. There was a huge teenage market ripe for exploitation, yet big business was, at first, strangely hesitant to take advantage of it. Company chairmen were keen to cash in on young people's spending power, but they also feared the new teenage affluence. They believed that it would make young people more assertive and independent, which in turn would bring about the collapse of age-old patterns of deference. Two sociologists who interviewed teenagers in 1963 found that over a third of the youngsters to whom they spoke expressed hostility to those in authority: 'I'd like to tell them to pipe down' and 'I do not like being ordered around' were typical replies.

The nervousness of the Establishment meant that the teenage market was initially exploited by young entrepreneurs rather than the more staid corporations. For example, in spite of the *Glasgow Sunday Mail*'s complaint that pop music 'monopolised' the airwaves, broadcasting organisations were reluctant to give it any airtime at all. Aware of a need that was not being met, Ronan O'Rahilly, manager of the Scene Club, moored an old ship ten miles off the Suffolk coast and installed a transmitter. On 28 March 1964 Radio Caroline went on the air. By May it had seven million regular listeners.

The government seemed powerless to act. When Labour came to office the Cabinet hummed and hawed about what was to be done. At a meeting of the Cabinet committee on broadcasting in May 1965 the postmaster-general, Anthony Wedgwood Benn (whose public image was one of youth and dynamism), proposed introducing legislation to ban Radio Caroline. Dick Crossman wrote in his diary that 'I was decisively against him on Radio Caroline because I didn't see any point in losing the votes of young people before the BBC had any real alternative to it.' There was a further delay, during which more stations began broadcasting. By the time the government introduced its bill to suppress the pirates, in summer 1966, there were at least eleven radio stations dotted around the British coast. In order to mollify the teenagers, the government asked the BBC to set up its own pop music channel, Radio One. Many of the disc jockeys hired for Radio One were taken from the pirates (especially from Radio London, which had been by far the most professional of the illegal stations), but somewhere in the transition from ship to shore their programmes seemed to have lost their excitement. Radio One, most youngsters felt, was extremely flaccid.

The role of youthful entrepreneurs in opening up the teenage market was especially noticeable in the world of fashion. Mary Quant had been an art student at Goldsmiths' College and had then worked for a time in a high-class milliner's shop. However, in her autobiography, Quant recalled that 'I had always wanted young people to have a fashion of their own, absolutely twentieth century fashion.' The young, she believed, 'were tired of wearing essentially the same as their mothers'. In November 1955 she opened Britain's first boutique, Bazaar, with money put up by her future husband, ex-public schoolboy Alexander Plunket-Greene. The shop was in the King's Road, Chelsea, which was at the time a

Glad to be thin: The ideal shape for a girl of the 1960s, according to designer John Bates, was 'narrow body, perfect square shoulders, long legs, small bust'. Twiggy, a Cockney sparrow weighing six and a half stone, had all this and more. She was nominated 'Woman of the Year'.

rather decaying, bohemian area. The first thing that struck Mary Quant was that she could not buy what she considered to be 'absolutely twentieth century' clothes for her shop, so she set about designing them herself, and hired a team of sewing-machinists to put her ideas into practice. Her bold, black-and-white designs sold well. Other boutiques, as well as coffee bars, began to open in the King's Road. By 1961 Quant was selling her designs wholesale. In 1963 she went into mass production to meet the growing demand, and started exporting to the United States. By then the mod cult was taking off; according to her own effusive account, 'it was the mods who gave the dress trade the impetus to break through the fast-moving, breathtaking, uprooting revolution'.

What Mary Quant did for women was repeated for men by another young boutique owner, John Stephen, a Glaswegian grocer's son who had come to London in 1956 when he was nineteen years old. After working as an assistant in Moss Bros, he raised enough money to open his own shop in Carnaby Street, Soho. He chose this fairly unprepossessing backstreet simply because the rents there were cheaper than anywhere else in central London. He was aware that it was still thought effeminate for men to dress flamboyantly and in order to counter this he hired exaggeratedly 'butch' figures, such as professional boxers, to model his clothes. He need not have worried. As we have seen, the mods had no inhibitions about the pleasure they took in their dress, and however daring some of John Stephen's clothes may have seemed—pink hipsters, for instance—there was no shortage of male teenagers willing to buy them. John Stephen's boutiques in Carnaby Street—by the early 1960s he had half a dozen of them—became a mecca for the serious mods, who would turn up every Saturday to see what new designs had appeared in the previous week. It was in Carnaby Street that The Who were kitted out in the correct style so that their manager could launch them as the first 'mod' pop group; The Who themselves were never quite as fastidious about their clothes as some of their fans.

The ambivalence with which many adults regarded this boom was mirrored by a number of teenagers. For the more dedicated mods, much of the attraction of their style had been that it was part of a secret war, a personal rebellion. Once it was mass marketed, it was bound to lose its original significance. The same feeling caused the mods to lose interest in the Beatles soon after they made it to the top; the Fab Four were accused of 'selling out'. As far as the mods were concerned, Beatle songs such as 'Help' were artificial compared with the 'genuine' anthems of frustrated youth which they heard when the Rolling Stones sang 'I Can't Get No Satisfaction' and 'Get Off My Cloud'—or, above all, when The Who performed 'My Generation', matching action to words as Pete Townshend rammed his guitar into its amplifier and Keith Moon battered his drum-kit into a rubble.

The mods' suspicions were confirmed by the direction which the fashion industry took. Carnaby Street, which they had come to think of as their territory, was invaded by tourists and television camera crews who wanted to inspect this symbol of Swinging London. By the time of the introduction of the mini-skirt, trends in young people's clothes were increasingly dictated by professional designers or the media, rather than by the teenagers themselves. This applied to other aspects of style: record companies tried to impose new dances such as 'the Carnaby', while a magazine grandly announced its invention of a 'new mod walk: feet out, head forward, hands in jacket pockets'. By the end of 1964 the original mods were calling themselves 'stylists' or 'individualists' instead, to dissociate themselves from the people who had, in their view, jumped on the bandwagon; even Lord Snowdon was described as a 'mod' when he appeared in public wearing a polo-necked shirt.

Although the purists were disgruntled, the teenagers who had discovered 'young fashion' slightly later than the first mods still

found it all a great thrill. This was especially true of middle-class girls. 'When I got my first mini-skirt,' says one, who was sixteen in 1964, 'I didn't think I would ever wear anything else.' And even though the fashions of Chelsea and Soho were becoming more broadly acceptable as they lost their subversive connotations and concentrated on 'fun', they were still too outlandish for some. John Bates, a designer who had won an award for producing 'The Smallest Dress in the World', was commissioned in 1965 to create a new wardrobe for Diana Rigg to wear in the television series *The Avengers*. Something bang up to date was required, and John Bates provided what was to become known as 'The Look'—bold black-and-white designs, with skirts well above the knee. ABC felt that the skirts were too short and surreptitiously tried to lower the hemlines. Bates retaliated by not putting hems on. The ABC cameramen, in a splendid last-ditch stand, claimed that their cameras were technically incapable of photographing such loud blacks and whites. Then they gave in.

Despite occasional digestive problems of this sort, the Establishment found itself able to swallow the new fashions without too much difficulty. Mary Quant aimed for a 'total look' which included make-up and handbags as well as clothes. The only part of the body for which she didn't cater was the hair, but this was adequately dealt with by Vidal Sassoon, a young man from West London who introduced new hairstyles with gusto. He was so successful that by 1965 he was opening a hair salon on Madison Avenue in New York; in the same year Mary Quant and other young British designers were invited across the Atlantic to show their work to the Americans. Another fashion designer, Barbara Hulanicki, opened a boutique called Biba in Kensington Church Street and extended the concept of the total look to include the decor of the shop itself, which was embellished with mahogany screens, potted palms and hat-stands.

In 1965 John Bates described the ideal shape for a '60s girl: 'narrow body, perfect square shoulders, long legs, small bust'. The following year someone was found who fitted the description perfectly—Twiggy, a seventeen-year-old flat-chested Cockney who weighed just six and a half stone. 'It's not what you'd call a figure, is it?' she remarked winningly. Soon afterwards she was named Woman of the Year. At the same time the OBE was awarded to Mary Quant, who went to Buckingham Palace for her investiture wearing a mini-skirt. The total look had been given the Establishment's blessing, like Merseybeat the previous year, and copies of designs from Quant and Biba appeared in department stores all over the country.

Early in 1967, just as middle-aged women were taking the plunge and daringly trying on trousers and short dresses, another change occurred. It had been anticipated by the switch in the type of drugs taken by young people. The mods had been confirmed believers in the merits of amphetamines (which speeded them up) and much of the style and music of the mods had been affected by this speed. By 1967, however, more and more young people were experimenting with marijuana (which slowed them down) and LSD (a hallucinogen). The qualities of the newly fashionable mind-expanding drugs were reflected in a single brought out by the Beatles in February 1967. One side of the record was straightforward enough—a pleasant Liverpudlian ditty called 'Penny Lane'—but the other side was decidedly odd. 'Strawberry Fields Forever' was a meandering, dreamy, spaced-out song which marked the beginning of the psychedelic boom; it was, significantly, the first Beatles single since 'Please Please Me' not to reach the top of the charts. It was followed in the summer by an LP which was even more peculiar—*Sergeant Pepper's Lonely Hearts' Club Band*, a *bouillabaisse* of Eastern mysticism ('Within You, Without You'), British music halls ('When I'm Sixty-Four') and drugs ('Lucy in the Sky with Diamonds'). The Beatles vehemently denied that there was any significance in the fact that the initials of 'Lucy in the Sky with Diamonds' spelled 'LSD', but it seemed too much of a coincidence to have been an accident.

Sergeant Pepper was released in June 1967, and throughout the summer psychedelia blossomed in a proliferation of antique regimental uniforms and cow-bells, beads and flowers. Those not prepared to go the whole way could compromise by wearing ruffled shirts and 'flower power' ties, preferably in the shape of the 'kipper tie' which was launched by Mr Fish, a fashion entrepreneur who owned a boutique in the King's Road.

Men's hair became longer and longer. A month after the release of *Sergeant Pepper* Scott Mackenzie's hymn to flower power, 'San Francisco', went to No. 1 in the singles charts on both sides of the Atlantic. In the same month, July 1967, the Beatles issued 'All You Need is Love', a song whose lyrics consisted almost entirely of the title being repeated over and over again. Not to be outdone, even the mean old Stones entered into the spirit of the summer of love, producing 'We Love You' in August. At the same time, Mick Jagger and Marianne Faithfull accompanied the Beatles on a visit to the Maharishi Mahesh Yogi, only begetter of Transcendental Meditation.

The hippies' ideology, if one can call it that, was a confused but alluring amalgamation of drug-taking, exotic religion, radical politics, pacifism and a desire to get 'back to nature'. The fascination with the mysterious East manifested itself in numerous ways. In spring 1968 the Beatles travelled to Rishikesh in India to study Transcendental Meditation at the Maharishi's academy. Ringo, always the most down-to-earth of the four, gave up after a fortnight; Paul followed him shortly afterwards, but John and George stayed for the best part of three months. George later transferred his affections to the Society for Krishna Consciousness, a cult to which he has remained impressively loyal ever since. George also became a great admirer of Ravi Shankar, a sitar player who was rather bemused to find himself elevated to international stardom as a result of the hippy boom. By August 1967 he was giving concerts in such large auditoria as the Hollywood Bowl. George Harrison, needless to say, flew over to America to cheer him on.

As the hippy culture gained popularity, more and more young people made pilgrimages to Marrakesh or Katmandu, partly because they believed they could 'get their heads together' by wallowing in Asian culture and partly because they were under the impression that drugs were available in unlimited quantities in that part of the world. Richard Alpert, a previously sober Harvard professor, grew a swami-like long white beard and insisted on calling himself Baba Ram Dass. A colleague of his, Timothy Leary, announced his conviction that LSD was the only true religion; he urged all young people to tune in, turn on and drop out. The growth of interest in Eastern mysticism also encouraged Western hippies to rediscover their own countries' older superstitions. In Britain, places with ancient magical connections—such as Glastonbury and Stonehenge—became fashionable gathering points; hippy magazines printed articles on ley-lines and earth gods.

The hippy culture was essentially an American invention, and the hippies' links with politics were much more discernible in the States than in Britain. Jerry Rubin, a young campaigner against the Vietnam war, was subpoenaed in 1966 to appear before the House Committee on Un-American Activities, an institution which had acquired notoriety in the 1950s when Joe McCarthy used it to conduct his witch-hunts against Communists. Rubin arrived for the hearings in Washington dressed in the uniform of a soldier in the American War of Independence, complete with brass buttons and buckled shoes—a harbinger of the gold-braided military outfits which began to appear in the Portobello Road in London the following year. Rubin was arrested for disorderly conduct, but his gesture had given him the idea for the Yippies (Youth International Party), which he founded with Abbie Hoffman in 1967. The aim of the Yippies, as described by Rubin was 'guerrilla theatre media politics'. In 1968 the Yippies held an 'alternative convention' outside the hall in Chicago where Democratic Party delegates were meeting to choose their presidential candidate. The alternative convention was graced by the presence of hippy gurus from the

Hippy horticulture: If you're going to San Francisco, one pop song exhorted, be sure to wear some flowers in your hair. And, it should have added, on your face, hands, feet and stomach. Sufferers from hay fever were unable to join in the fun at summer 'love-ins'.

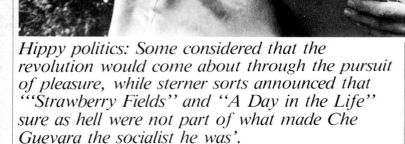

Hippy politics: Some considered that the revolution would come about through the pursuit of pleasure, while sterner sorts announced that "'Strawberry Fields" and "A Day in the Life" sure as hell were not part of what made Che Guevara the socialist he was'.

older generation such as William Burroughs and Jean Genet, but on the very first night it was broken up by police armed with tear-gas and clubs. As Jerry Rubin put it, 'Yippies are hippies who've been hit on the head by policemen.'

In America, the hippies were able to ally themselves with new radical groups such as the Black Panthers or the student movement (particularly the Weathermen, a guerrilla faction in Students for a Democratic Society). Although there was some tension between the American hippy movement's druggy wing and its political wing, it was not so pronounced as that in Britain. In 1968, when the British left-wing paper *Black Dwarf* was preparing to bring out a special issue to celebrate the Grosvenor Square demonstration against the Vietnam war, Mick Jagger sent the paper's editors a hand-written copy of the lyrics to 'Street Fighting Man' as a token of solidarity. Not all the comrades were impressed by this, or by John Lennon's public support for the paper. One reader of *Black Dwarf* described Jagger as 'an unfortunate nothing whom the world could do well without', while Lennon was dismissed as 'a poor confused drug experimenter'. Another reader wrote that 'there is not anything in Lennon's thinking that hunger and a few weeks in Fidel's canefields would not correct . . . "Strawberry Fields" and "A Day in the Life" sure as hell were not part of what made Che Guevara into the kind of socialist he was.'

The antagonism was mutual. The *International Times*—an underground paper which, like *Oz*, had started life in 1966—had nothing but contempt for the 'Communists, socialists, professional discontents and black-power advocates' who protested in Grosvenor Square in 1968. They were people who 'would rather march and talk about it than think and act effectively'. The paper explained what it meant by effective action:

> *International Times* favours Design Revolution, Spiritual Evolution, Ying-Yang Uprising, Inner Space Adventure, Work Democracy, a Release of Man's Extraordinary Potential and the Transformation in the Myths that direct Life and Thought.
>
> If you really want to travel why can't you just transfer yourself—by changing your matter into energy and back again? Why can't you? What's stopping you from doing it?
>
> The answer is in your head!

Similarly constructive statements were made by many hippies in the late 1960s. On 20 March 1969 John Lennon and Yoko Ono were married in Gibraltar; they then went to the Hilton Hotel in Amsterdam, where they spent their one week's honeymoon in bed, giving non-stop press conferences to 'protest against world violence'. Their Hilton suite was covered with placards which read 'Stay in Bed', 'Grow your Hair!', 'I Love Yoko', 'Hair Peace' and 'Bed Peace'. The couple sent 'acorns for peace' to a hundred world leaders, and announced that the idea of protesting by staying in bed was henceforth to be known as 'bagism'. The next appearance of bagism was supposed to take place at Freeport in the Bahamas, but when they arrived at the hotel John and Yoko discovered that the rooms had only twin beds, which were cemented to the floor. Undeterred, they gathered their entourage and flew to Montreal, where they began a ten-day 'bed-in for peace' at the Queen Elizabeth Hotel. While in bed they gave at least sixty interviews to journalists; they also wrote the song 'Give Peace a Chance' and had a mobile sound unit brought to their bedroom so that they could record it. Apart from John and Yoko, other singers on the record included Timothy Leary and the Canadian branch of the Radha Krishna Temple.

This mixture of radicalism and spaced-out freakiness reached its zenith later in 1969, when Lennon gave back his MBE. In letters to the Queen and the prime minister, Lennon wrote: 'I am returning this MBE in protest against Britain's involvement in the Nigeria-Biafra thing, against our support of America in Vietnam and against Cold Turkey slipping down the charts.' The letter was signed: 'John Lennon of Bag.'

Unlike teds and mods, the hippies were mostly middle class. The life of working-class youths in the Fifties and Sixties had the same structure as that of their parents, with a clear boundary between work and leisure. The mods may have claimed to be mods twenty-four hours a day; but that was mainly a description of a state of mind. After a hard night's dancing on Sunday they would still be at school or in the factory on Monday morning. Jobs were unsatisfactory but inescapable. The mods and the teddy boys accepted, like their parents, that work was a necessary evil that provided the money with which they could 'escape' in their spare time.

The hippies had a quite different set of assumptions. Coming from middle-class homes, they had been led to believe that work was more than simply a means of paying the mortgage; it was something that ought to be satisfying as well. They had been brought up to think of 'careers' rather than 'jobs'—an important distinction. Moreover, middle-class youths had longer in which to ponder their future. Whereas working-class children would leave school at fifteen and start work straight away, middle-class youngsters tended to stay on at least until A-Levels. Many would then spend another three or four years taking a degree, and even those who didn't go to university might do something else for a year or two—voluntary work overseas, perhaps—before entering the rat race.

The hippies were, therefore, able to go much further than the mods. They felt that a truly dissident youth culture involved nothing less than the creation of an alternative society, to be set apart from the existing one—an idea which the 'alternative convention' in Chicago had shown in microcosm.

There was never any coherent blueprint for an alternative society. Hippies chased the dream in various ways. Some 'dropped out' altogether, pursuing their utopian ideal through drugs, mysticism and rural self-sufficiency—ingredients which came together in songs such as Steve Miller's 'Journey From Eden'. This lifestyle was especially popular in the United States: by 1970 there were several thousand communes in America, while Britain had about fifty.

Other hippies did not cut themselves off from society so completely. They stayed in towns and tried to keep in touch with 'the people', but they rejected the existing institutions. Jim Haines, a young American who delighted in staging 'happenings', founded the Arts Lab in London. Although the idea of experimental theatre predated the hippy movement—Charles Marowitz had begun his Theatre of Cruelty in 1964—much of today's alternative cultural scene, such as fringe theatres and arts centres, owes its success to the infusion of energy and ideas which the hippies brought.

Another effect of the hippies' activities can be seen in the current trend towards healthier eating. Most hippies, with their 'back to the earth' beliefs, found frozen food and hamburgers unpalatable. In 1969 the organisers of the Woodstock festival in America served raw oats—'the first hippy granola'—to the assembled multitude of 400,000. As one of the hippy caterers remarked, 'it was a struggle to get them down, but if you did it was good for you'. Hippies in Britain also believed that natural foods were good for you, but many of them found it was a struggle to buy them: conventional shops were devoting less and less of their space to unprocessed food. For those hippies who had retired to country communes there was no problem—they could grow their own. Urban hippies decided that the only solution was to set up their own shops, which would sell neglected commodities like whole wheat or organically grown vegetables. These shops attracted the attention—and the custom—of other town-dwellers who were not hippies. By the 1980s there was hardly a town in Britain which did not have a health food store.

In many other respects, too, the hippies did succeed in creating an alternative society within the existing one. For British companies the 1960s was the period of the merger boom, when the credo that big is better went almost unchallenged by politicians and industrialists. The hippies thought otherwise, and they set up innumerable cottage industries in crafts such as weaving or printing. By the 1980s conventional opinion had come round to accepting the hippies' view. Small firms and workers' cooperatives enjoyed an unprecedented vogue, and politicians went out of their way to denounce the faceless, monolithic corporations which, in the 1960s, they had helped to create.

Another of the hippies' achievements was the squatting movement which combined some of the characteristics of the rural utopians—such as drugs and communal living—with political activism. The legacies of this have been considerable. Housing action groups and 'resource centres' flourished, and most of the community groups of today contain a sizeable percentage of ex-hippies. Organisations which were founded during the hippy boom, such as Friends of the Earth or Release, became increasingly professional; they hired lawyers and researchers, and presented evidence to Royal Commissions.

This change was reflected in the underground press. In the late 1960s *Oz* and *IT* were usually colourful rather than committed, more interested in freakiness than in, say, campaigns to improve public housing. By 1971, however, exclamation marks and exotic lay-out were no longer thought to be sufficient. Two new papers were born: *Seven Days* was a left-wing news magazine while *Ink*'s declared intention was to 'provide space for the kinds of story that journalists were frequently aware of but afraid to publish'. Both these ventures were short-lived but another radical paper with hippy connections, *Time Out*, went from strength to strength. In America *Rolling Stone* and *Village Voice* both acquired huge circulations with a mixture of rock criticism and serious political reporting.

It was all a long way from wop-bop-a-loo-bop. And although few middle-class teenagers were unaffected by the spread of hippy culture, working-class youths were less impressed. In 1965 they had still been able to go to their local club and see the Yardbirds or the Animals. By 1969 rock groups had become grand and distant, performing in great stadiums or at huge open-air festivals. What was more, the music had changed: you could hardly dance to the Soft Machine. Even the old idols had gone soft. The Rolling Stones had produced *Their Satanic Majesties Request*, their own version of *Sergeant Pepper*, while The Who had created a ninety-minute rock opera, *Tommy*. Ironically, it was Yoko Ono who told *Rolling Stone* in 1972 that 'the folk music of the age, Pop Song, is becoming intellectualised and is starting to lose its original meaning and function.' Yet Yoko Ono and John Lennon were themselves far from innocent of the offence.

Working-class youths first showed their disaffection with this development in July 1969, when the Rolling Stones gave a free concert in Hyde Park. A gang of youngsters came and jeered. It was the public debut of the skinheads.

Considering that skinheads have normally been associated with racism, it is interesting to note that their style was inspired by black people. We have already seen how British mods in the late Fifties and early Sixties were responsible for the upsurge of interest in black rhythm and blues, an interest which led to the creation of the Beatles and the Rolling Stones. But the black music of the late '50s also found an enthusiastic audience in Jamaica, where local musicians soon introduced a slight but important modification—'ska'. The difference was that in rhythm and blues the emphasis fell on the downbeat, whereas in ska it was on the upbeat, giving a jerky, exciting effect. Chris Blackwell, the son of a white plantation owner in Jamaica, formed a company called Island Records to capitalise on the cult.

Blackwell's success in the West Indies persuaded him to bring ska to Britain. Several British cities had large communities of Jamaicans, who had emigrated to Britain with their young children

Let it all hang out: 'If you really want to travel why can't you just transfer yourself — by changing your matter into energy and back again? Why can't you? What's stopping you from doing it? The answer is in your head!' A helpful suggestion from the International Times

in the 1950s. The youngsters were now in their teens, and in a state of some cultural confusion. Their attitude to Jamaica was slightly similar to that of an adopted child towards its real parents. They wanted to discover more about the homeland from which they had been so suddenly removed years before. The arrival of ska gave them a chance to do so. They took to the new music eagerly, and adopted a style to go with it—that of the 'rude boys'.

Although one ska record did make the hit parade—Millie's bouncy song 'My Boy Lollipop' in 1964—most of the music was, at first, bought only by rude boys. However, the rudies' style—sharp clothes, pork-pie hats, jive talk—soon caught the attention of the appearance-conscious mods. It struck them as being the epitome of super-cool. As early as 1964 some mods were wearing their hair closely cropped, in admiring imitation of the short, 'fuzzy' hairstyles of the West Indians. These 'hard mods' also sported braces, another trade mark of the rude boys.

By about 1966 ska had turned into rocksteady, which had a much more pronounced bass sound. This was the form which, a few years later, became known as reggae. Although rocksteady was slower than ska, it was still good for dancing. Many white working-class youths certainly found it preferable to 'Lucy in the Sky with Diamonds', and they spent their evenings mingling with young rudies in the West Indian clubs of south London.

The skinheads were thus heavily influenced by the new Jamaican culture. However, paradoxically, they also believed that they were reaffirming what they saw as the traditional attitudes of the white working class—racism, conservatism and a contempt for the middle classes. The skinheads' uniform resembled that of the rudies; but, with its braces and heavy boots, it was also an exaggerated version of the dress of a stereotypical white manual worker. West Indians were acceptable because they were, in the skinheads' view, 'just like us'—rough and alienated. For Asians, however, skinheads had nothing but hatred. 'Paki-bashing' rapidly became one

All you need is love: 'He walks — no, runs — into this shop and buys me a box of matches! What could I do with a bleeder like that but hit him? ... Have you seen the way they grovel *round you, the way they're always trying to please you? I hate them, that's all.'*

of the favourite pastimes. Des, a young Birmingham skinhead, gave an illuminating account of the skins' mentality:

I'll tell you why I hate the bloody Paks. I'll tell you a story. A week or so ago I was walking down the street with a couple of mates. I wanted a light for my fag, so I walk up to this Paki git and ask him: 'You got a light, mate?' And what do you think the fucker did? I'll tell you. He walks—no, runs—into this shop and buys me a box of matches! Now, I ask you! What the fuck could I do with a bleeder like that but hit him? And another thing. Have you ever been in their restaurants? Have you seen the way they *grovel* round you, the way they're always trying to please you? I hate them, that's all. (Quoted in *Rock File*, 1972.)

The skinheads' racism was, in other words, a continuation of the class war by other means. The West Indian immigrants were thought to have allied themselves with the working class. But the Asians—all of whom were called 'Pakis'—had aspirations to join the middle class.

Similar attitudes dictated the skinheads' hostility to middle-class white youths who, the skins believed, were undermining traditional working-class versions of masculinity. 'Hippy-bashing' and 'queer-bashing' were depressingly common, and just as the term 'Paki' was used to describe anyone from the Indian sub-continent, the word 'queer' was applied to any man who had long hair or frilly clothes.

Even the skinheads' special relationship with the young West Indians did not last long. In the late Sixties and early Seventies jobs were becoming harder to find, and doubly so for young black people because of the racial discrimination shown by many employers. Finding Britain inhospitable, young Jamaicans began yearning for home—not in the West Indies but in Africa. During the early 1960s the cult of rastafarianism had grown enormously in Jamaica, and its main belief was that black people's true home was in Africa, whence they had been forcibly removed by slave traders. The rastafarian leader Marcus Garvey had told his people that a black king in Africa would lead them to deliverance. This was later interpreted as referring to the Emperor Haile Selassie of Ethiopia; rastafarians revered him as the Living God and the Lion of Judah (also known as 'jah'). There would be no end to black people's 'sufferation' and 'slavery' in Babylon (the land of exile) until they

TILES CLUB, OXFORD STREET, 1967 (PHOTO: BBC HULTON PICTURE LIBRARY)

Ska and skins: 'There was that song "Young, Gifted and Black" by Mike and Marcia, and when we played it all the skinheads used to sing "young, gifted and white" and they used to cut the wires to the speakers and we had some fights and less white people used to come...'

returned to their spiritual home, Ethiopia.

This religion was adopted by many Jamaican teenagers in Britain in the late Sixties and early Seventies. They had their hair plaited in dreadlocks, and they took to wearing woolly caps knitted in the colours of the Ethiopian flag. Their music changed too, becoming much more openly political. Apart from 'The Israelites', a rastafarian song by Desmond Dekker and the Aces which topped the British charts in May 1969, appreciation of the new reggae was almost exclusively confined to young West Indians. The skinheads had turned to West Indian music because they could no longer identify with their earlier heroes such as the Rolling Stones. But now West Indian music was cutting itself off from them too, as it became more concerned with black consciousness and a new religion which the skins found baffling. They became angry and bitter, as one young West Indian told the *Sunday Times* in 1973:

> There was that song 'Young, Gifted and Black' by Mike and Marcia, and when we played it all the skinheads used to sing 'young, gifted and white' and they used to cut the wires to the speakers and we had some fights and less white people used to come up after that.

Having rejected white music as well, the skinheads had nowhere left to go. Music was relegated to a position of minimal importance in their lives. They devoted their energies instead to attending football matches, where they sought to recover the excitement and crowd loyalty that they had once found in rock and reggae.

The skinheads' extreme disillusion was shared, to a lesser extent, by thousands of other young people. During the first half of the 1970s rock music reached absurd levels of pomposity and overkill. Groups released double or triple albums instead of three-minute singles. Concerts were performed not in small, sweaty clubs but in gigantic arenas equipped with light-shows and dry ice. It was not until 1976, with the arrival of punk rock, that another generation of teenagers was able to re-create the spontaneity of twelve years before. The vitality of the first beat groups on Merseyside, and of the Rolling Stones and The Who in their early days, had come from the closeness between audience and performers. As Keith Moon had said of Who concerts, 'the people who come along identify themselves with us. They look at us on stage and think they're like us.' Before the 1960s were over the Stones and The Who were driving around in limousines and living in country mansions. The punk explosion of 1976 was an attempt to give new life to Keith Moon's idea. The punk bands made a virtue of the fact that they weren't expert musicians, and that their amplifiers left something to be desired. Tens of thousands of teenagers responded.

Punk groups were determined not to go the same way as their predecessors in the mid-'60s. Some of them succumbed to the temptations of wealth, of course, but many, such as The Jam, remained impressively true to their original intentions. The Jam's heroes were the early mod groups, but they went to enormous lengths to show that they didn't intend to lose touch with their audience as their ancestors had done. This attitude clearly made some of those ancestors feel pretty uncomfortable. In 1982 Pete Townshend of The Who wrote an open letter to the Jam's leader, Paul Weller, in *Time Out*. Townshend began by praising Weller's desire not to become too grand or remote: 'He is genuinely concerned that anyone who identifies with his feelings should not be let down. He has no large expensive car, shuns large houses . . .' Eventually the strain became too much, and Townsend concluded: 'Paul, buy yourself a big car mate. You're one of the few people in this country who deserve one.' The youth of the '80s had picked up the long-discarded banner of the '60s, and one of the people who had first waved that banner told them to throw it away.

POLITICS

'We felt we had to out-trump the Tories by doing what they would have done'
Richard Crossman, Labour minister, 1965.
'You notice how we only win the World Cup under Labour?'
Harold Wilson.

'This is our message for the Sixties,' Harold Wilson declared at the Labour Party conference in October 1960. 'A socialist-inspired scientific and technological revolution releasing energy on an enormous scale.' But it was by no means clear that the British people wanted any such revolution. Only a year earlier, in October 1959, they had returned Harold Macmillan's government to office with an increased majority—the Conservatives' third successive general election victory. It was not hard to see why.

In a speech in 1957 Macmillan had commented: 'Indeed, let's be frank about it, some of our people have never had it so good.' In later years this remark was used against him; critics suggested that it showed the old man's complacency, his aristocratic ignorance of social problems. In reality, however, Macmillan was speaking the truth. Between 1920 and 1940 unemployment had never fallen below one million. From 1945 until the end of the 1960s it never rose above it (except momentarily during a fuel crisis in 1947). With full employment had come an age of remarkable prosperity. Between 1950 and 1959 the cost of living increased by 47 per cent, but the growth in wages easily outstripped this: a manual worker's average earnings rose by 80 per cent in the course of the decade.

People had jobs; they also had more money than ever before. At the last Cabinet meeting before the 1959 election Macmillan passed round copies of the latest issue of *Queen* magazine, which had taken as its theme one word—'BOOM'. The aim of the magazine was to extol Britain's new affluence:

Nearly two thousand million pounds is pouring out of pockets and wallets and handbags (the gold mesh one above costs five guineas from Jarrolds) and changing into air tickets and oysters, television sets and caviar, art treasures and vacuum cleaners, cigars and refrigerators. Britain has launched into an age of unparalleled lavish living.

The fact that Macmillan thought this worthy of his ministers' attention suggests that he considered it a good testimonial to his government's achievements.

Not everyone shared this view. In its issue of 2 January 1960 the *New Statesman* described the 1950s as a cynical, materialistic and selfish decade, in which the existence of workhouses, mental institutions and overcrowded classrooms 'was concealed in the public mind by a flood of cars, TV sets, spin-driers and hire purchase gimmicks. "I'm all right Jack" became a way of life, a national anthem. It was a Tory decade.'

Whether one approved or disapproved of the boom of the late 1950s, no one could deny that it happened. It's important to stress

this, because there is a tendency today to view the political history of the Fifties and Sixties in a dangerously over-simplified way. Between 1951 and 1964, so the theory goes, Britain was ruled by the Conservative Party under a succession of aged and aristocratic rulers—Churchill, Eden, Macmillan, Douglas-Home—who were out of touch with the modern world. In 1964, the theory continues, the British people rejected the decaying upper-class government and embraced Harold Wilson, the young, dynamic, thoroughly modern grammar-school boy.

This is a highly misleading interpretation. It was only in its last couple of years that the Conservative government's public image was that of being a collection of clapped-out country gentlemen. In the late 1950s the Conservatives presented themselves, with some success, as being rather more 'modern' and 'go-ahead' than the Labour Party. In 1958 Britain entered the jet age with the launch of the Boeing 707 and the Comet IV; in the same year London's first tower block was built; and in 1959 Britain's first motorway was opened. Meanwhile, after the Labour Party's defeat in the 1959 general election, the Labour leader Hugh Gaitskell suggested that the party should change its name to something with a more 'twentieth-century' image. Labour, he felt, was too closely associated in the public mind with flat caps and working men's clubs, and not with the fast new technological age. His feelings were echoed by a market research study in 1961 which found that Labour supporters thought the Tories exercised a much greater attraction for ambitious people, middle-class people, young people, office workers and scientists. 'The image of the Labour Party,' the study concluded, 'is one which is increasingly obsolete in terms of contemporary Britain.'

How did the ailing Labour Party of 1960 become the 'dynamic' party of 1964? And how did the Conservatives make the same transition in the opposite direction? The simple answer is that they didn't. What changed was not the ideas or practice of the parties, but the rhetoric and image. Harold Macmillan had been filling his Cabinet with aristocrats for several years, but no one had thought this fact to be especially noteworthy. By the early 1960s, however, a new generation of journalists and politicians (most of them Labour supporters) were beginning to expound upon the 'need for change' and they fastened on Macmillan's penchant for the upper class, in the belief that it would serve to discredit him. Anthony Sampson's book *Anatomy of Britain*, published in July 1962, actually included a full-scale family tree which was designed to show how many of Macmillan's relations held important public offices.

Those who wished to discredit the Conservative government in

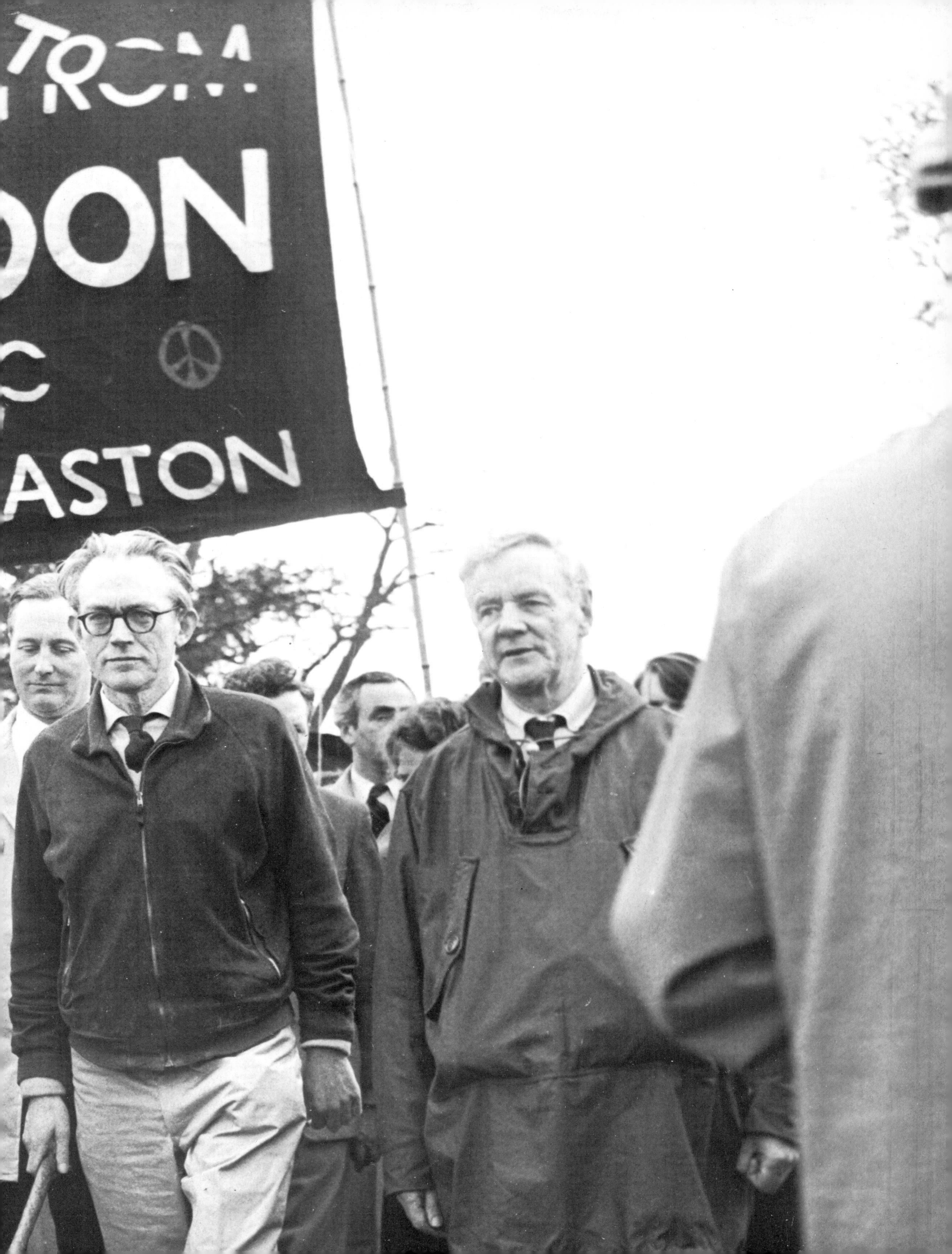
FROM
DON
ASTON

this way cannot have foreseen how well events would play into their hands. The Profumo scandal, which broke in 1963, had only the most tenuous links with the aristocracy. None the less, the essence of the scandal—that war minister John Profumo had had a brief affair with a girl called Christine Keeler, who had also been friendly with a man called Ivanov from the Soviet Embassy—was quickly neglected as the press wallowed in articles about the 'decadence' of the upper classes (who, by implication, were probably related to the prime minister). As Richard Ingrams, the editor of *Private Eye*, later said: 'In the climate of 1963 it was enough for someone to be a Duke or Duchess for them to be associated in the public mind with Mr Macmillan and his cabinet.' Because Christine Keeler had first met Profumo at Lord Astor's home, Cliveden, the press ran stories about 'orgies' at Cliveden. There were also persistent rumours about a party in Bayswater at which a Cabinet minister had served dinner while wearing nothing but a mask and a bow-tie.

The scandal delivered a severe blow to the government's image. It was disfigured still further when, in October 1963, Harold Macmillan resigned on grounds of ill health. The obvious person to succeed him was R. A. Butler, an intelligent and respected politician. Instead, Macmillan nominated as his successor the 14th Earl of Home, who had been plucked from obscurity only three years before to become foreign secretary.

Orgies galore: In 1963, following a spate of sex scandals, Harold Macmillan retired and made way for the Earl of Home. 'After half a century of democratic advance,' Harold Wilson complained, 'the whole process has ground to a halt.' But by 1964 Wilson was in Downing Street.

As the Conservative government lumbered awkwardly towards the general election, the Labour Party was beginning to pick up speed. The Labour leader Hugh Gaitskell had died suddenly in January 1963, to be succeeded the following month by Harold Wilson. By the end of the year the contrast between the leaders of the two main parties could not have been more striking. Douglas-Home came across as a quaint but anachronistic laird ('I lived among miners for twenty years,' he said in October 1963, but most people found this pretty implausible). Wilson presented himself as an energetic young man who would sweep out the cobwebs; he fondly compared himself to President Kennedy.

Wilson's image came as something of a surprise to those who had known him since his early years in politics. At Oxford he had been a member of the Liberal Club. In 1944 he was selected as Labour candidate for Ormskirk in Lancashire. Shortly after this he bumped into Edward Jackson, an active socialist whom he had known at university. 'I'm standing for parliament,' Wilson told him. 'Really?' replied Jackson. 'For which party?' After he was elected to Parliament in 1945 Wilson gained the same reputation that he had had in the civil service during the war—that of an extremely competent but rather colourless administrator. The *Financial Times* was reflecting a generally held view when it suggested in 1950 that 'Mr Wilson is a pedestrian Parliamentarian. . . Deprived of administrative opportunity, Mr Wilson's star would be reduced to a faint flicker in the political firmament.' What had not occurred to the *Financial Times* was that Wilson's very colourlessness—the fact that he was not actively offensive to either the Left or Right of his party—might be the key to his success.

Wilson's brilliance as a political manipulator began to be fully appreciated only after he had been elected leader of the Labour Party in 1963; but the clues to it had been apparent for some time.

MANDY RICE-DAVIES GOES ON HOLIDAY TO MAJORCA, 1963

HAROLD AND MARY WILSON AT GREATER LONDON COUNCIL ELECTION, 1964

Throughout the late 1950s the Labour Party was bitterly divided between the left-wing supporters of Aneurin Bevan and the right-wing Gaitskellites. Harold Wilson was the only senior Labour politician who managed to straddle both sides, appearing at the Tribune rally at party conferences while simultaneously promising Gaitskell his whole-hearted support. The two issues which most divided the party were nationalisation and the H-Bomb. Wilson dismissed the former as a 'sterile argument', and made sure that he didn't commit himself too irrevocably to one side or the other. A telling account of his intentions was given at a private dinner in 1957 with the editor of the *Sunday Express*, John Junor, where Wilson praised Harold Macmillan with these words: 'The man's a genius. He's holding up the banner of Suez for the party to follow, and he's leading the party away from Suez. That's what I'd like to do with the Labour Party over nationalisation.' On the other bitterly contentious issue—disarmament—Wilson simply kept his head down. 'I leave foreign affairs and the H-Bomb to Bevan and Gaitskell,' he told the *Evening Standard* in 1959.

Wilson found a simple way of dragging the Labour Party away from its quarrels. He became a passionate advocate of science—a subject which could simultaneously unite the party (for who could dispute that science was A Good Thing?) and rid it of its old-fashioned cloth-cap image. In 1957 he told his constituents that 'it is the task of all of us to ensure that the great triumphs of the scientist are controlled by mankind in such a way as to bring happiness and not fear to all the peoples of the world'. Who could possibly disagree?

By the time he actually became leader of the Labour Party, in 1963, Wilson had developed his theme. His speech at the party conference that year—where he spoke of the 'white heat of technology'—has since passed into legend. Read on the printed page today it may seem vague and unoriginal, but to the members sitting in the conference hall in Scarborough in 1963 it was exactly what they wanted to hear. He began by giving them a tour of the wonders of modern technology, describing computers which 'do their calculations and take their decisions in a period of three millionths of a second'. He then proceeded to draw conclusions from this:

> First, we must produce more scientists. Secondly, having produced them we must be a great deal more successful in keeping them in this country. Thirdly, having trained them and kept them here, we must make more intelligent use of them . . . Fourthly, we must organise British industry so that it applies the results of scientific research more purposively to our national production effort.

The delegates roared their approval and, the following day, even right-wing newspapers could scarce forbear to cheer. It was new, it was exciting and it was wonderfully uncontroversial. Wearied by their internal battles and frustrated by twelve long years out of office, party members were thankful that at last they had something which could unite them. A general election had to come soon and Wilson had given them a message which could be presented to the electorate with genuine excitement—the prospect of a New Britain 'forged in the white heat of a technological revolution'. Both the Left and the Right within the party convinced themselves that Wilson had shown that he was on their side.

The election, when it came, was rather an anti-climax. Labour received fewer votes than at any general election since 1945, but due to the oddities of the British electoral system it also won more seats than at any time since 1945, and was able to form a government. It is worth emphasising that, despite the low vote, Labour's election campaign—with its slogan 'Let's Go With Labour'—did stimulate real enthusiasm among socialists, particu-

Harold Wilson: According to George Brown, 'if the film of Walter Mitty hadn't come first, Harold Wilson must have been the prototype on which that mythical character was based. His fantasies are endless.' Wilson compared himself to, among others, the Duke of Wellington.

larly young people. Having been out of office since 1951, Labour had no recent record to defend, and many of the children of the post-war baby boom had an innocent faith in the party's slogans. Even the *New Left Review*, a Marxist paper well to the left of Labour, praised the party's policies as being 'designed to produce an economy that is progressively more efficient and uses its resources more rationally than the one we have been used to'. There was nothing very Marxist about that, of course—running the capitalist system more 'efficiently' was a social democratic proposition normally derided by those on the left—but the euphoria created by Wilson was so infectious that even the far Left was prepared to suspend its critical faculties.

A more dispassionate appraisal of Labour's proposals before 1964 would have revealed that a Wilson government would inevitably turn out to be a disappointment. Matters which would be regarded as centrally important by most socialists—public ownership and the redistribution of wealth—were relegated to the margin. There was a specific promise to nationalise the steel industry (a promise that was eventually kept), but the chief idea seemed to be that the magic of technology would, by itself, create a better society.

Another danger was that a new Labour government would be fatally handicapped by Wilson's obsessive desire to keep the pound strong, whatever the cost. When James Callaghan became chancellor of the exchequer in October 1964 he found himself presented with a balance of payments deficit of £800 million, the largest in British history, which had been run up by the Tories to pay for their pre-election economic boom. The obvious solution was to devalue the pound, but Wilson would have none of it; devaluation became known as 'the unmentionable' among his ministers. His views on the subject ought not to have occasioned much surprise, since he had always shown himself to be as doughty a defender of the pound as any Conservative. In 1956, as shadow chancellor, he had told Parliament that 'it is the duty of all of us to put first the strength of sterling'. He didn't merely *support* parity of the pound; he believed that it took precedence over every other issue. He made this perfectly plain in a speech in 1958: 'The Labour Party, no less than the Conservative Party, gives defence of the pound the first priority . . . We shall need to sacrifice all other considerations to make sterling strong.' It seems that to Wilson the pound was important not for economic reasons but for reasons of national pride. He appears to have believed that if the pound were devalued the image of Britain would be devalued too.

This is borne out by Dick Crossman, a Cabinet minister and one of Wilson's confidants, who kept a diary throughout the 1964–70 Labour government. It is an invaluable account of the contrast between Wilson's image of the government—and of himself in particular—and the actual realities. Only a month after Labour took office Crossman recorded a significant encounter with Wilson in the dining room of the House of Commons. 'You know, Dick,' Wilson said, 'in any great campaign like the Peninsular War the commanding general has to know where to retreat to. He has to have his lines of Torres Vedras.' Crossman pointed out that the most useful retreat would be to devalue—a move which was supported by all three of Wilson's chief economic advisers. 'You're talking nonsense,' Wilson replied. 'Devaluation would sweep us away. We would have to go to the country defeated. We can't have it. No, I have my lines of Torres Vedras which I am retreating to.' What he meant by this, it later transpired, was that he was going to ask the governor of the Bank of England to raise £3,000 million to 'save' the pound. As Crossman observed, 'defending the pound by frantic cuts and then in the end finding one has to devalue makes no sense at all'. But this is exactly what happened. Wilson clung to his beloved sterling for three long years before he was forced to accept the inevitable. One Sunday evening in November 1967 he appeared on television to announce the devaluation of the pound.

Wilson's picture of himself as the Duke of Wellington in the Peninsular War was but one of a number of fantasy roles which he assumed in the Sixties. One of his Cabinet colleagues, George Brown, later wrote that 'if the film of Walter Mitty hadn't come first, Harold Wilson must have been the prototype on which that mythical character was based. His fantasies are endless. The roles he allots himself are breathtaking.' Advertising and public relations

were two of the boom industries of the 1960s, both of them concerned with creating an 'image' regardless of whether it bore much relation to the reality of the product. Harold Wilson was an appropriate leader for such an age.

Wilson took his lead from across the Atlantic. In 1960 John F. Kennedy was elected President of the United States on a skilfully created wave of enthusiasm (especially in the press) for his youth, his energy, his New Frontier politics and his promise of one hundred days of dynamic action. For the Labour Party, eager to shed its old-fashioned image, he provided a striking example of the way forward. In a party political broadcast a few months before the 1964 election Wilson specifically compared himself with Kennedy and emphasised the need for 'a hundred days of dynamic action' to get a 'stagnant' country moving again. In Britain, as in America, journalists were captivated by this exciting talk and were only too happy to help the young leader put his 'image' across. After the 1964 election two reporters, Richard West and Anthony Howard, produced a book called *The Making of the Prime Minister* whose title was a deliberate echo of Theodore H. White's adulatory study of Kennedy, *The Making of the President*.

Once he actually became prime minister Wilson dropped the Kennedy image for much of the time, but it never quite disappeared. Just before the 1965 party conference Dick Crossman challenged Wilson on the subject, telling him that 'any idea of our being a Kennedy regime is absurd'. 'I suppose you're right, Dick,' Wilson replied. 'You can't really sell a Yorkshire terrier as a borzoi hound.' Yet only a month later, when Rhodesia declared UDI, Wilson repeatedly referred to the problem as 'my Cuba'—a reference to Kennedy's showdown with Khrushchev during the Cuban missiles crisis of 1962. And in spring 1970, shortly before his government was replaced by the Tories, Wilson gave a series of parties at No. 10 Downing Street. 'Y'know,' Wilson said at one of them, surveying the assembled guests, 'there are people here from all walks of life—artists, musicians, sculptors. Jack Kennedy's parties at the White House had nothing on this!'

The common factor in these widely contrasting roles was that they were an attempt by Wilson to invest himself with a populist glamour, to link himself to people who might not normally be thought to have much of a connection with politics. The guest lists for his Downing Street parties provide a fair guide to the types of people to whom Wilson hoped to appeal. There were fashionable artists and intellectuals, represented by painter David Hockney, pop artist Alan Aldridge and novelist Iris Murdoch. There were upwardly mobile and ambitious people such as the advertising executive David Kingsley and Jack Straw, President of the National Union of Students. Finally there were those who were supposed to represent working-class culture—television comedians Morecambe and Wise, and various professional footballers.

Wilson was always conscious of the need to suggest that he had the common touch. In private he liked to smoke cigars and drink brandy but these tastes, evocative of boardrooms and country houses, were not indulged in public. Instead, he chewed reassuringly on a pipe. His wife, Mary, told the press of Wilson's fondness for smothering his food in HP Sauce, and Wilson himself proudly showed off his ability to recite from memory the French inscription which appears on HP Sauce bottles. One remarkable manifestation of his 'ordinary bloke' persona came when England won the World Cup in 1966: Wilson flew back from talks with President Johnson in America so that he could be present at the Cup Final, and he made a point of having himself photographed with the victorious English team. 'Have you noticed how we only win the World Cup under a Labour government?' he said some years later, at a footballers' dinner. He meant it only half-jokingly. Wilson always believed in the importance of being seen as a figurehead of British popular culture, and even his colleagues seem to have fallen

Protest power: In The Importance of Being Ernest, *Lady Bracknell said that if education had any effect 'it would probably lead to acts of violence in Grosvenor Square'. During the 1960s successive demonstrators headed for the American embassy there. Not all were violent.*

HAROLD WILSON WITH SIR ALF RAMSEY, ENGLAND'S FOOTBALL MANAGER (PHOTO: BBC HULTON PICTURE LIBRARY)

Football fan: 'It was a tremendous, gallant fight that England won,' wrote one of Wilson's colleagues after the World Cup victory in summer 1966. 'Our men showed real guts and the bankers, I suspect, will be influenced by this.' Wilson apparently thought so too.

under his sway in this respect. On the day after Britain's victory Dick Crossman wrote in his diary that the World Cup had given Wilson's personal standing a huge boost, and

> could be a decisive factor in strengthening sterling . . . It was a tremendous, gallant fight that England won. Our men showed real guts and the bankers, I suspect, will be influenced by this, and the position of the government correspondingly strengthened.

In political terms the government might be in difficulties but as long as the population was provided with entertainment—and the government was seen to be connected with that entertainment—Labour might yet hang on to office. The point was put with embarrassing honesty by David Kingsley, the advertising executive who ran the advertisements for Wilson and the Labour Party (and who gave his services free of charge). Interviewed by the *Sunday Times* just before the 1970 general election Kingsley gave it as his opinion that Harold Wilson's 'greatest achievement' had been his appearance on *Sportsnight with Coleman*.

David Kingsley was as responsible as anyone for creating the image of Harold Wilson and his party in the 1960s. He created the slogan 'Let's Go With Labour' for the 1964 election and the 1966 line 'You *Know* Labour Government Works'. His *Sunday Times* interview is worth quoting at some length for its unintended revelation of the barrenness, the self-deception and the shabby opportunism which characterised the Labour government between 1964 and 1970.

Speaking in the excitable language favoured by ad-men, Kingsley began with a breathtaking statement.

> Ideals are coming back. They're the now thing. This is an interesting thought that has only just occurred to me—we could really sell the Labour Party on ideals in the present climate of opinion. I don't think, in practical terms, we could have talked about them in '64 and '66.

To Kingsley—and, by implication, the government which he advised—ideals were apprently no more than a gimmick, like a free gift in a cornflakes packet, which could be added or left out according to the state of the market. The truth of the matter was quite the reverse. The 1964 Labour government *had*, in some ways, been 'sold' on ideals; certainly a number of young people had worked enthusiastically for Labour's victory. By 1970 many of them, feeling betrayed and disillusioned, had given up on the Labour Party. It would have needed more than a slick advertising campaign to convince them that they were wrong.

If other people felt disillusioned after six years of Labour government, Kingsley betrayed no sign of it.

> Do you travel the country? It's fantastic to go up North, to Tyne-Tees, Manchester, Leeds and Birmingham. Quite incredible what a difference these six years have made. Men driving taxis just tell you about it, not knowing who you are or anything, they just want you to know how happy they are. It's the new buildings, and the roads, mainly.

Having conjured up this preposterous scene, Kingsley sails blithely on.

> This change in the country that marked the Wilson era has made the whole world notice us: it started with the pop music, Swinging London bit. The technological breakthrough has helped . . . Our continuing economic crisis, which kept us in the news, helped too, of course.

OVERLEAF: WORK IN PROGRESS ON THE M1, BRITAIN'S FIRST MOTORWAY

Here the ad-man's mentality is revealed: anything which keeps the eyes of the world upon us can't be bad.

Kingsley is well into his stride by now.

> It is impossible for ordinary people to say 'we're not better off these days'. The Child Poverty Action Group people talk about the really poor, and quite right they are to do so. But such folk have come on in the Wilson era, they just haven't come on quite as much as other people.

This was an astonishing admission of defeat, disguised by Kingsley to sound like success. The Child Poverty Action Group and other campaigners had not suggested that the poor had become poorer in *absolute* terms, i.e. that someone earning £10 a week in 1964 was earning £9 a week in 1970. What they did say was that under Labour the poor had become *relatively* worse off—that the gap between rich and poor had actually widened. Under a Labour government supposedly committed to the redistribution of wealth, the people who did best were those who were already doing pretty well anyway, while the people who fared worst were those in the greatest need.

Most socialists would consider this to be a failure. Kingsley does not, and he produces a wonderful catch-all explanation of his view: 'The old days, when governments made things happen—lovely idea—are over. Now prime ministers cope with things as they arise, and government is a management task.' To Dick Crossman, who observed the government from the inside, this was apparent almost from the beginning. On 13 December 1964, less than two months after taking office, he wrote in his diary: 'I'm not sure we have done very well in terms of our own socialist strategy . . . I get the impression this government isn't running itself in but just running along.' By the following June he felt no more cheerful: 'Here we are, drifting along, with our momentum halted and the civil service taking over more every day.' In September 1965 Crossman read a draft of a conference speech in which Wilson intended to talk about introducing the New Britain and then to add: 'Here we have stepped forward and done it.' Crossman turned to Wilson and told him: 'But we haven't done it. That's the trouble. And people know we haven't.'

David Kingsley would have answered Crossman by saying that governments cannot 'make things happen'. His belief that government is no more than a 'management task' is enormously revealing about the politics of the Wilson era, for it is essentially a civil service idea. During the Fifties and Sixties government could be presented as simply a 'management task', a matter of ensuring that everything was running smoothly. In the 1950s the word 'Butskellism' was coined to suggest the lack of any serious difference between Hugh Gaitskell, Labour's chancellor, and his Tory counterpart, Rab Butler. In the 1960s the term 'MacWilsonism' would have been equally appropriate as a way of describing the relative similarity—behind their rhetoric—of the Tory and Labour governments. It is highly significant that Wilson has seldom missed a chance to proclaim his enormous admiration for Harold Macmillan. Both men represented the kind of politics that the civil service likes—the kind that doesn't look like politics. A telling example of Wilson's attitude came in a 1967 television interview in which he declared that 'I would like to see defence, as far as possible, taken out of politics'. By asking for defence to be taken out of politics Wilson was, in effect, saying that his own defence policy was not a socialist one but that he didn't wish to admit it; instead, therefore, he tried to pretend that defence was a 'non-political' matter, as the civil service would have us believe.

Vietnam, immigration and strikes were three issues during Wilson's term of office which provided good illustrations of his *modus operandi*. In the early 1950s Wilson was a stern critic of

Let's go with Labour: 'Ideals are coming back. They're the now thing. This is an interesting thought that has only just occurred to me — we could really sell the Labour Party on ideals in the present climate. I don't think ... we could have talked about them in '64.'

WOMEN AT LABOUR PARTY CONFERENCE, 1966

American policies on Indo-China. 'It must be the duty of the British Parliament,' he said in 1952, 'and the British Labour movement in particular, to make it clear that if any section of American opinion sought to extend the area of fighting in Asia, they could not expect us to support them.' Two years later, at a May Day rally in Liverpool, he announced that 'we must not join with nor in any way encourage the anti-Communist crusade in Asia, whether it is under the leadership of the Americans or anyone else'. Leaving no room for doubt about his position, he added: 'Asia is in revolution and Britain must learn to march on the side of the peoples in that revolution and not on the side of their oppressors.'

Once he was in office, Wilson showed no sign of remembering that he had ever taken such a stand. When American planes bombed North Vietnam in 1965 Wilson told the House of Commons that, 'as I have said many times before', he wanted to make it 'absolutely plain' that his government gave its full support to US policy 'against Communist infiltration' in Vietnam. In the 1950s Wilson had argued forcefully that people in Indo-China ought to be allowed to express their views through elections. By 1965, however, he was telling Parliament that 'conditions were not there for an election'. The magazine *Private Eye* cruelly but accurately pictured Wilson's position with a drawing by Gerald Scarfe which showed Wilson with his tongue hanging out, pulling down President Johnson's trousers at the rear in order to lick his backside. The caption read: 'Vietnam: Wilson right behind Johnson.'

LBJ was duly grateful for Wilson's unqualified support. On Wilson's first trip to Washington after becoming prime minister, Johnson had been distinctly cool. After Wilson had given his full backing to the Vietnam war, however, the special relationship blossomed. Returning from a trip in December 1965 Wilson reported 'complete agreement' between himself and the president. The love affair reached even greater heights in July 1966. At a lunch in Washington Johnson proposed a toast to Wilson by comparing his courage with that of Churchill in the Second World War:

> I must say that England is blessed now, as it was then, with gallant and hardy leadership. In you, sir, she has a man of mettle. . . Your firmness and leadership have inspired us deeply in the tradition of the great men of Britain.

In Britain itself many people were less enthusiastic: despite pleas from George Brown, the then foreign secretary, the 1967 Labour Party conference rejected the government's position on Vietnam.

Two years earlier, in June 1965, Wilson had tried to placate opponents of his Vietnam policy by unveiling his idea of a Commonwealth Peace Mission. The plan was that Wilson would head a team of five Commonwealth leaders who would go to Hanoi and Peking to try to arrange a ceasefire. The scheme was doomed from the start. Wilson, whose government was already publicly committed to supporting the United States in the war, was hardly likely to be accepted by the Communists as an honest broker. Moreover, the plan had the 'warm support' of President Johnson, and its most enthusiastic advocate at the 1965 Commonwealth Conference was Sir Robert Menzies of Australia; as Wilson himself conceded later, 'no world leader more strongly supported the American Vietnam policy than Sir Robert'. China instantly dismissed Wilson's idea as a US-backed 'hoax'; the *People's Daily* of Peking described Wilson as a 'nitwit'. When it became clear that North Vietnam and China would not receive Wilson's mission, it was suggested that President Nkrumah of Ghana should go on his own, since he was acceptable in the Communist capitals. Wilson discouraged this idea, since Nkrumah was an opponent of America's involvement in Vietnam and, as Wilson said, 'I feared the line he might take.'

Hey, hey, LBJ: In the 1950s Wilson had said that it was the duty of the Labour Party 'to make it clear that if any section of American opinion sought to extend the area of fighting in Asia, they could not expect us to support them'. By the 1960s he was right behind Uncle Sam.

So, within weeks of its creation at the 1965 Commonwealth Conference, Wilson's peace mission was dead. It had been backed by the Americans, the Conservative Party and the *Daily Mail* ('It is an exciting idea for which . . . Mr Wilson must be given the full credit') but any intelligent observer could have seen that it would be a non-starter. Why, then, had Wilson proposed it? Dick Crossman, who considered the scheme a 'political stunt', gives an intriguing account of a conversation with Wilson soon after the mission had been stillborn.

'I really was anxious, Harold,' said Crossman, 'that if this stunt had come off you might have been away for a whole month.'

'Oh, I don't think it would have been a month,' Wilson replied. 'At the most it would have been a fortnight. Anyway, I think we have got most of the value we can out of it already.'

Wilson's last sentence made Crossman wonder whether the real motivation behind the idea of a peace mission was the prospect of the Commonwealth Conference breaking up on the first day as a result of a furious row over Rhodesia. 'In order to postpone that row and create a better atmosphere,' Crossman thought, 'Harold needed a personal initiative on the first day, and in this sense I have no doubt the stunt was brilliantly successful.' In short, Wilson was only too happy to propose action which would cost him nothing and would achieve nothing, while he was not prepared to do something which might have had some effect but would have risked offending an ally—the issuing of an outright public condemnation of American involvement in Vietnam. To criticise America would have been 'political'; to support America was nothing more than 'management'.

The same attitude—taking highly political decisions, but dressing them up to look otherwise—is visible in the Wilson government's record on immigration. Until Harold Wilson became the Labour leader, his party's policy on Commonwealth immigration had been straightforward: Commonwealth citizens were British subjects, and they therefore had the right to come to Britain and settle there if they wished. Labour's spokesman on Commonwealth affairs, stating the party's position in the House of Commons in 1958, had been unequivocal: 'We on this side are clear in our attitude towards restricted immigration. We are categorically against it. The central principle . . . is the "open door" to all Commonwealth citizens.' In 1961, when the Conservative government introduced a bill to restrict Commonwealth immigration into Britain, Hugh Gaitskell, Labour's right-wing leader, opposed it passionately. Wilson said soon afterwards that this fight was 'one of the greatest of the many inspiring acts of Hugh Gaitskell's leadership'. Yet when Wilson himself succeeded Hugh Gaitskell as leader in 1963 he introduced a marked change in the party's attitude, telling Parliament that 'we do not contest the need for control of Commonwealth immigration into this country'. The principle for which Labour had previously fought so hard had been unceremoniously ditched; now, Wilson's only argument with the Tories was about the fine details of their policy.

The controls introduced by the Conservatives in 1962 saw a dramatic fall of black immigration to Britain from 136,000 in 1961 to 51,000 in 1964. None the less in March 1965, only five months after taking office, Wilson told the House of Commons that the Tories' Act was 'not working as intended', and consequently a 'fresh examination of the whole problem of control' was necessary. In his memoirs of the period Wilson gives an extremely brief account of his action, saying merely that there was 'a justifiable concern in all parties' about the number of immigrants who were entering the country 'through the widespread evasion of existing statutory controls, by fake passports, impersonation and false or unfulfilled statements'. This gives the impression that Wilson was cracking down only on those who were illegally evading the existing controls; but the truth of the matter is that Wilson actually extended those controls. The annual quota of work vouchers issued to Commonwealth workers was cut from 20,000, to 8,500 and vouchers for unskilled workers were abolished altogether. Immigrants' dependants also had their rights of entry reduced. The Labour Party, which until two years previously had opposed the whole concept of restricting Commonwealth immigration, was now behaving more harshly than the Tories had done. At that year's Labour Party Conference an emergency motion demanded

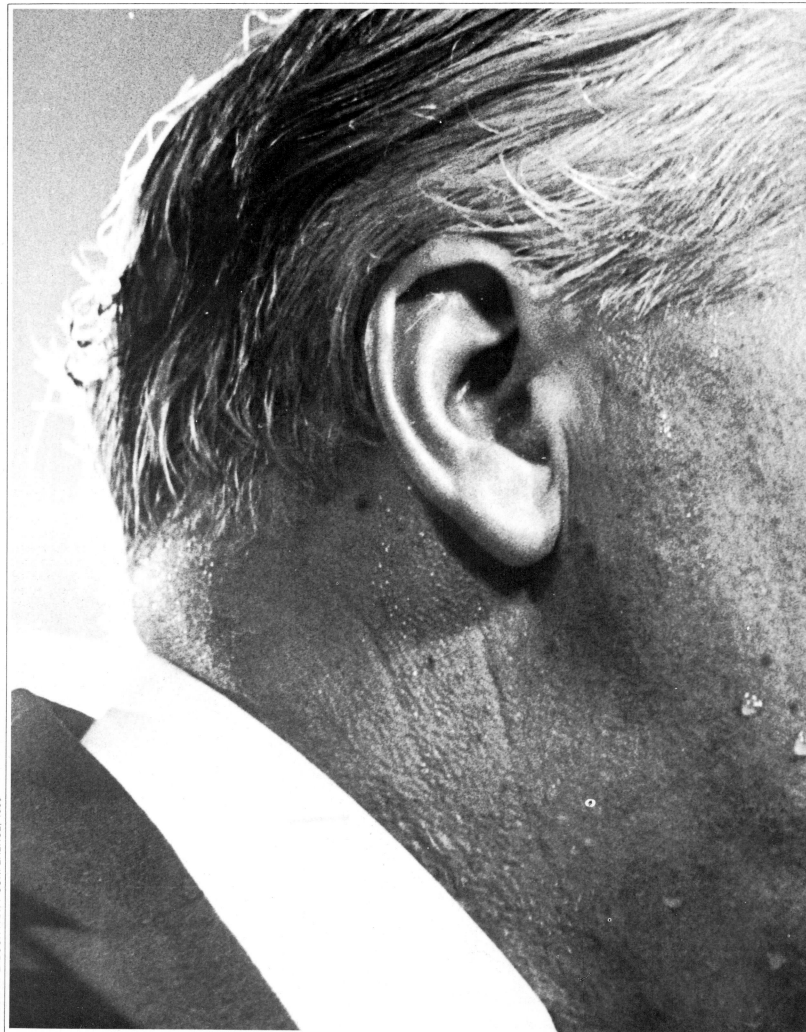

WILSON AT LABOUR PARTY CONFERENCE, 1966

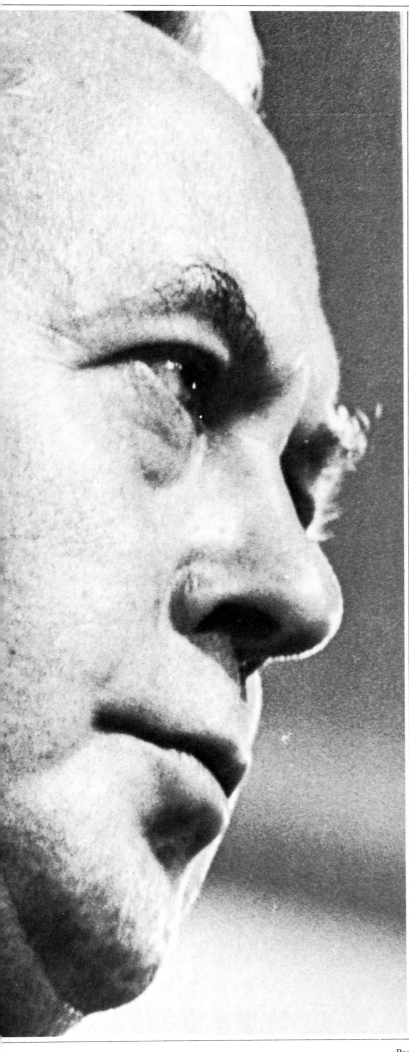

that Wilson should withdraw his proposals; it received one and a half million votes but was defeated. Wilson gives a telling one-sentence description of the conference argument: 'There was a major row over our immigration policies, about which a very wide section of party opinion, understandably, felt very strongly.' If Wilson found it understandable that a very wide section of his own party should be disgusted by his behaviour, why did he not pause to consider whether, perhaps, he might be in the wrong?

The answer is a deeply cynical one. Wilson's Cabinet *knew* that they were in the wrong. They realised that their immigration White Paper was immoral and unsocialist—but they went ahead with it. In a most illuminating passage in his diary, Dick Crossman explained their reasoning:

> This has been one of the most difficult and unpleasant jobs the government has had to do. We have become illiberal and lowered the quotas at a time when we have an acute shortage of labour. No wonder all the weekend liberal papers have been bitterly attacking us. Nevertheless, I am convinced that if we hadn't done all this we would have been faced with certain electoral defeat in the West Midlands and the South-East. Politically, fear of immigration is the most powerful undertow today . . . any attempt now to resist demands for reduced quotas would have been fatal. We felt we had to out-trump the Tories by doing what they would have done and so transforming their policy into a bi-partisan policy.

Labour feared that there was a growing number of racialists in Britain, whose votes might be crucial in some marginal constituencies. The government had a clear political choice. It could stick to its principles and take an honest stand against the racialists, explaining why they were wrong. Or it could give in to the racialists in the hope of gaining their votes, while at the same time trying to placate its own supporters by presenting the move as another mere 'management task' which had no connection with politics. It unhesitatingly picked the latter course.

The government's record on immigration went from bad to worse. Like other East African leaders, President Kenyatta of Kenya was pursuing a policy of 'Africanisation' in the mid-1960s, which meant discriminating against his country's non-African residents—particularly those of Indian origin. At the time of Kenyan independence in 1963 the British government had given the Asians in Kenya a choice between taking Kenyan citizenship or keeping their British status. Over 150,000 decided to stay British, having been given a specific assurance that this would entitle them to come and settle in Britain if they ever wished to do so.

Towards the end of 1967 several racialists on the right of the Conservative Party, notably Enoch Powell and Duncan Sandys, suggested that Britain was about to be 'flooded' with Kenyan Asians fleeing from Kenyatta's persecution. Many Kenyan Asians were deeply alarmed that the government might act on Powell's suggestion and 'shut the door' on them. As a result, they did indeed begin to come in greater numbers: in the first two months of 1968 no fewer than 12,800 Asians were admitted. Once again, Wilson's government was faced with a simple choice. It could reassure the Kenyan Asians by stating unequivocally that their right to come to Britain was not in jeopardy; this would undoubtedly have prevented any sudden, panic-stricken influx from taking place while also making it clear that the government intended to honour its obligations to those who did wish to come. Instead, however, Wilson and his colleagues decided to confirm the Kenyan Asians' worst fears. At the end of February 1968 they introduced their Commonwealth Immigrants Bill, which, for the first time in history, removed the right of certain British citizens to live in Britain. It was an unashamedly racialist measure: no one, not even

Tough at the top: 'It was widely felt,' Crossman wrote later, 'that our improved majority in 1966 was due to our new tough line on immigration.' The Times *described Wilson's immigration law as 'probably the most shameful measure' ever introduced by a Labour government.*

OVERLEAF: CND RALLY IN TRAFALGAR SQUARE, APRIL 1965

in the government, pretended that they would have acted in this way if the British citizens had been white instead of black. In a newspaper article some years later Dick Crossman explained that

> it was widely felt that our improved majority in 1966 was due to our new tough line on immigration control. That is why as a government we were panicked in the autumn of 1967 . . . and began to make contingency plans for legislation which we realised would have been declared unconstitutional in any country with a written constitution and a supreme court.

Yet again, the government was concerned solely with hanging on to its parliamentary majority, whatever the cost.

The bill—which *The Times* described as 'probably the most shameful measure that Labour members have ever been asked by their whips to support'—was rushed through Parliament in three days by the home secretary, James Callaghan. The Conservative Party officially abstained and the bill was passed without difficulty although 35 Labour members voted against it and many more abstained. It is worth noting that 10 Liberal MPs and 15 Tories also opposed the Bill.

On 20 April 1968, less than two months after the passing of the Act which his scaremongering had inspired, Enoch Powell made a speech in Birmingham. 'We must be mad, literally mad,' he said, conjuring up a nightmarish vision of a breakdown in social order caused by mass immigration: 'Like the Roman, I seem to see the River Tiber foaming with much blood.' The following day he was sacked by the Tory leader, Ted Heath, who called the speech 'racialist in tone and liable to exacerbate racial tensions'. Hundreds of London dockers and meat porters marched to the House of Commons in support of Powell. It later transpired that this 'spontaneous' demonstration had been carefully organised by members of the recently formed National Front, but this was hardly the point: racialism had become a fully-fledged political force.

By its anti-immigrant actions in 1965 and 1968 the Labour government had implicitly accepted the argument that black immigrants were a dangerous threat to British society. It is hardly suprising that many ordinary people followed the government's lead, or that mass-circulation newspapers began to run stories with titles such as 'They're Swamping Us!' After all, had not the prime minister admitted as much?

In the light of this, Harold Wilson's own account of the matter deserves full marks for audacity. In his memoirs he attacks Ted Heath, incredibly, for *not* instructing Tories to vote against the 1968 bill. This, Wilson believes, was the point at which 'many liberal-minded Conservatives decided to break with Mr Heath . . . From then on the Monday Club took over the guardianship of the Tory conscience.'

His discussion of Enoch Powell's 'rivers of blood' speech is even more astonishing.

> What I noticed with sadness in the months and years ahead was that however deep the personal bitterness between him and Mr Powell, Mr Heath seemed on the run in terms of policy and successively adopted tougher attitudes, on some issues following Mr Powell's line with a delay of three to four months.

Wilson intends no irony: he seems genuinely to have forgotten that he himself followed the Powell line, with only the briefest of delays, by introducing the Commonwealth Immigrants Act of 1968. Wilson continues:

> Mr Powell's words, and Mr Heath's equivocation towards his attitudes—while attacking his language—became an important political factor. It was not so much that Alf Garnett for the first time became a political figure in his own right [Garnett was a parody of a working-class racist, who appeared in the BBC's comedy *Till Death Us Do Part*] . . . What Mr Powell had done for the first time was to make him politically articulate and to confer upon him a degree of political respectability.

Wilson again neglects to mention that his own government had shown no compunction about making racialism respectable.

Wilson has always professed his hatred of racialism. In 1958 he called colour prejudice 'a blot on our national life' and in 1964, when a Tory named Peter Griffiths had been elected as MP for Smethwick after fighting a particularly nasty racialist campaign, Wilson declared that Griffiths should be treated as a 'parliamentary leper'. These words cost Wilson nothing and achieved nothing. But when he had the opportunity to provide a lead and set the tone of the national debate about race relations, notably in 1965 and 1968, he capitulated to the racialists. No less a figure than the Archbishop of Canterbury had said that the 1968 Act would do irreparable harm to race relations, and subsequent events proved him correct. Inside Parliament, successive governments followed Wilson's example and introduced increasingly draconian immigration rules, culminating in the Conservatives' 1981 Nationality Act. Outside Parliament a number of parties sprang up on the far right, breeding on the disaffection of white youths with their economic lot; in parts of the country many black families lived in a state of virtual siege. Enoch Powell's forecast of rivers of blood—like his suggestions that Kenyan Asians would come to Britain—became a self-fulfilling prophecy, when in 1980 and 1981 violent rioting broke out in several British cities. Obviously Harold Wilson did not foresee what would happen in the Seventies and Eighties; but it is nevertheless true that by its actions his government identified immigrants as being 'the problem' and, in the minds of many people, the impression stuck.

Wilson's immigration policies lost him much support on what might be called the intellectual right-wing of the party—the sort of people who belonged to the Fabian Society and who, although they were right-wing on subjects such as economics or disarmament, had always prided themselves on the liberal decency of their views on social issues and race relations. One such figure, Nicholas Deakin, resigned from the Labour Party in 1968 shortly before he was due to stand as a Labour candidate in the local elections. He accused Wilson's government of 'bungling, cynicism, opportunism and malice' with regard to its Commonwealth Immigrants Bill.

The Left, too, were sickened by Wilson's stance on immigration, but their disillusionment also encompassed Labour's failure to take a stand against the Vietnam war. Indicative of their feelings was a letter to *Tribune* in August 1965 by Malcolm Caldwell (who was, fourteen years later, to meet his death in Cambodia). Caldwell wrote:

> Socialist principles have been tossed aside with almost indecent cynicism and casualness. Racial discrimination in Britain has been condoned and strengthened. American butchery in Vietnam has been actively supported and encouraged . . . It is a sad picture and I can personally neither see nor offer any excuses.

By the end of 1965 the Labour Party had thus alienated a significant proportion of its most active middle-class members—the young idealists on the Left and the rather older Fabians on the Right. It is probably true to say, however, that issues such as immigration and Vietnam had less of an effect on Labour's supporters in the industrialised working class; this certainly seems to be borne out by the impressive 110-seat majority which Labour won over the Conservatives in the election of March 1966. For working-class voters the turning point came in summer 1966, when Harold Wilson demonstrated that a Labour government could be every bit as bullying and hostile towards workers as any Tory administration. The huge disaffection which followed showed up clearly in the opinion polls: in May 1966 Labour had a lead of 15½ per cent over the Conservatives; by November 1966 this had been whittled away to nothing.

Two things had happened between these polls: Wilson had succeeded in breaking a strike by seamen; and Labour's commit-

Statesmanlike: At a lunch in Washington in 1966 President Johnson told Wilson: 'I must say that Britain is blessed now ... with gallant and hardy leadership. In you, sir, she has a man of mettle ... Your firmness and leadership have inspired us deeply in the tradition of Britain.'

Wilson and the workers: When the traditionally moderate seamen went on strike in 1966, Wilson denounced the strike's organisers as 'a tightly-knit group of politically motivated men'. He hinted at Communist subversion, but gave no evidence. The strike collapsed soon afterwards.

ment to the welfare state had been called into question.

The National Union of Seamen (NUS) was a traditionally moderate union, which had not been on strike for fifty years. In 1965 the union's negotiators had agreed to a 56-hour week, but only on the understanding that this allowed ships' masters to call on seamen to work at any time *within* these 56 hours. It had not been envisaged that seamen would actually work the full 56 hours, but a number of shipowners had started to insist on it. By spring 1965, the seamen were, not surprisingly, keen to renegotiate the agreement. They demanded a 40-hour week and a 3s rise in their basic weekly pay (which was under £15). The employers refused—on the advice of Ray Gunter, minister of labour, who was determined that the seamen's claim should not succeed. The seamen decided to go on strike. On 13 May, just before the strike was due to begin, Wilson summoned the entire 48-strong executive of the seamen's union and warned them of the damage they would do to the nation. Their reaction, in Wilson's own words, 'was militant and bitter and with many offensive comments on the shipowners' methods, and their excessive profits, and with political attacks on us for backing the bosses against the workers'. By 16 May the strike was in full swing: no British ships were putting out to sea. Wilson broadcast to the nation, announcing that it was 'the duty of the government' to resist the strike, for it was 'a strike against the state'. By 23 May, with the seamen determined to hold fast, Wilson was advising the Queen to declare a state of emergency. The pound fell to its lowest level for over a year. On 26 May an official inquiry was set up under Lord Pearson to examine the seamen's case; its report, published two weeks later, recommended delaying the introduction of a 40-hour week. The seamen rejected it.

On 20 June Wilson made a statement to Parliament in which he said that the strike had started as 'a naturally democratic revolt, which is now giving way, in the name of militancy, to pressures which are anything but democratic'. The strike, he continued, was being organised by a 'tightly-knit group of politically motivated men, who, as the last general election showed, utterly failed to secure acceptance of their views by the British electorate'. He did not mention the word 'Communist', but no one doubted that this was what he meant. However, even newspapers which were normally only too happy to run 'red scare' stories, found themselves hampered by Wilson's failure to produce any evidence.

Eight days later he did his best to assist them by giving a long speech in which he named the members of the 'tightly-knit group'. It was pretty unconvincing stuff, not least because Wilson was forced to concede that not a single member of the union's executive was a Communist, and it was the executive which had sanctioned the strike. Nevertheless, it contained enough sinister-sounding allegations—such as a reference to two seamen staying in a Communist's flat—to create an atmosphere of suspicion and unease among the strikers.

Tony Wailey, a Liverpool seaman at the time, gives a vivid account of the effect of Wilson's remarks:

All day it was Communist this and Communist that. You looked over the hut and Eddy had his face stuck in a newspaper and he still told them to get stuffed but his voice wasn't so big, so Cavanagh gets up and shouts the creeps down and Eddy looks up and laughs, then one of the creeps turns quick and says why doesn't he go back to bloody Russia, and there's damn near a fight and the ganger comes in and even if he's Eddy's cousin he's not looking too pleased. And it's strange the way everything was all right up until Wilson made his comments . . . And it's the same on the picket lines; people are shouting down at you from buses and you couldn't remember that before. And you swear you see and hear that bloody word communism more times in the next few days than you've ever done in your life.

The union's executive, most of whom were not militants, were deeply unnerved by Wilson's attack. At the first executive meeting after Wilson's speech the right-wingers moved that the strike be called off at once. The Left proposed that there should be a ballot of the entire union membership but the Right, aware that most seamen were still solidly behind the strike, outvoted them. The strike was over, and the men were ordered back to work.

The seamen's strike, like miners' strikes, had occupied an especially romantic place in the heart of the Labour movement. The seamen were thought of as brave men who risked their lives on stormy oceans and were paid a pittance for it. When their strike got under way they had offers of solidarity from the dockers and other groups of workers. When the strike was broken, it was not only the seamen who felt betrayed. (The dockers' sense of betrayal was compounded the following year when they staged a strike of their own. Once again Wilson and Gunter blamed it on the Communists, and once again no serious evidence was produced.)

Wilson had hoped that the ending of the seamen's strike would have stopped the run on the pound, but in fact the selling of sterling continued unabated. Although he blamed it on 'moaning minnies' and 'the sell-Britain-short brigade', he clearly had to do something. He could either devalue the pound or take money out of the economy. At this stage he was still clinging resolutely to his refusal to devalue so instead, on 20 July 1966, he announced a package of the most deflationary measures in Britain since the war—huge cuts in public spending, a credit squeeze and a legally binding wage freeze for six months (which would, he promised, be followed by very strict controls on pay rises).

If there was any one moment when the Labour government lost the loyalty of the working class, this was it. Working-class families felt the effect of Wilson's measures in their pocket, since there were to be no pay increases. They felt it in their lifestyle, since Wilson's credit restrictions affected hire purchase, the method by which most working-class people bought consumer durables such as cars and televisions. They felt it in the reduction in public services, such as the closing of swimming pools. And some of them felt it in a more direct way, since Wilson's squeeze put thousands of people out of work. A few months after Wilson's initial measures insult was added to injury, as prescription charges were pushed up to 2s 6d and free milk was abolished in secondary schools. Ironically enough, Wilson had himself resigned from a Labour Cabinet in 1951 over the imposition of National Health Charges. By 1967 he appeared to see no incongruity in presiding over a government which re-imposed them.

Working people's anger was directed not only at the Labour government but also at the trades unions. During the Sixties and Seventies more and more union leaders were sucked into a tripartite corporate state consisting of government, management and unions. They were given jobs on quangos, they were invited to serve on Royal Commissions and, in general, they were asked to see themselves as responsible, statesmanlike people. In 1968, on the 100th anniversary of the founding of the Trades Union Congress, the Queen herself invited 900 trades unionists to a Buckingham Palace garden party, where she expressed the hope that 'you will continue to provide the wise leadership on which our country so much depends'. Such flattery and coddling were highly successful. As we have seen with the seamen's dispute, when Wilson made his accusation of Communist manipulations the union's leaders were aghast, even though they must have known that the allegations were false. What upset them was the idea that they should be thought of as dangerous militants (despite the fact that their claim was hardly an excessive one). They had to find a way of showing that they were respectable people after all, and the only way which they could think of was to call off the strike.

By 1968 workers were becoming increasingly frustrated to find,

At the barricades: As the 1960s progressed, politics took to the streets in ways unparalleled in living memory. The uprising in Paris nearly toppled the French state in 1968, while pitched battles in Northern Ireland the following year caused the British government to send in troops.

when they went on strike, that a senior official from their own union, usually from a distant head office in London, would come down and order them back to work. They began to put their faith in shop stewards and 'rank and file committees', which were made up of people from the workplace concerned and were therefore much more directly in touch with the mood of the workers. There was a growing number of 'wildcat' or unofficial strikes which were staged in defiance of the union bosses in London, who seemed too busy consuming beer and sandwiches at Downing Street (or tea and cakes at Buckingham Palace) to carry out the traditional functions of trades unionists.

In January 1969 Barbara Castle, minister for employment and productivity, sought to restore some 'order' to union affairs by publishing her White Paper *In Place of Strife*, which proposed that ministers should have the power to order a 28-day 'cooling off period' during which strikers would have to return to work. Ministers should also have the power to order a ballot of all members involved in any disputes.

This was too much for the TUC, who had always considered the 'policing' of union members to be their job and not that of the government. After waging a determined campaign, they forced the government to back down—but only because of a TUC promise that they themselves would enforce rigorous discipline on unofficial strikers. As Harold Wilson put it in his memoirs, the TUC's 'fire-fighting machinery' was just as effective as government powers in ensuring that workers behaved themselves. The glee with which union leaders carried out this task confirmed the argument put by a striking building worker in London two years previously: 'An alliance was formed between the employer, the state and right-wing trade union leaders.'

A good example of the bitterness engendered was provided by the strike at Pilkington's glass factory in St Helen's, Lancashire, in 1970. What started as an argument over mistakes in wage packets rapidly turned into a full-scale walk-out, much to the horror of the union concerned, the NUGMW. A rank-and-file strike bulletin of 10 May 1970 gave a flavour of the workers' feelings:

Brothers and sisters: We have now come to the parting of the ways. The NUGMW no longer serves any useful purpose for the workers of Pilkington. Therefore . . . we are issuing the forms for contracting out of the NUGMW. By so doing we rob Pilkingtons of the last argument they have for not conceding our claim, that is, that the NUGMW think their offer 'fair and reasonable'.

A bulletin three days later included a poem addressed to the union's general secretary, Lord Cooper:

Little Lord kneels at the foot of the bed
Looks underneath to see if there's a Red.
Hush, hush, whisper who dares,
Little Lord Cooper is saying his prayers.

The scansion may leave something to be desired, but the sentiments were deeply felt.

Another indication of the mood of the time was given by Jim Lamborne, a car worker involved in the Ford dispute of 1969: 'This strike is about control. We, the ordinary workers' want to control our unions. Never again' will we allow eighteen stiff-necked bureaucrats to make agreements in our name against our interests.'

For all Lamborne's brave talk of 'never again', agreements 'against our interests' were made again and again over the succeeding decade. Employers and ministers were eager to flatter union leaders into acquiescence, and to turn poachers into gamekeepers. An especially remarkable example of this came in 1981 when Reg Brady, a union official at Times Newspapers who had led a one-year lock-out, was suddenly appointed to the Times management—as head of industrial relations. When James Callaghan was prime minister in the late 1970s he complained that union leaders were not exercising 'enough control' over their members; general secretaries fell over themselves to assure him that this was not true. To have suggested that a more natural order might be the other way round—that the members of an organisation ought to control

potential of this mass . . . [The] changing social function of higher education has been reflected in the introduction of new subjects—in particular social sciences—which encourage the student to understand and participate in the apparatus of social control . . . In Britain, as elsewhere, it is often these students who most militantly reject the roles offered to them.

The first signs of disquiet manifested themselves at the London School of Economics (LSE), an institution which was soon to become synonymous with sit-ins, lock-outs and all the other paraphernalia of student rebellion. In summer 1966 Dr Walter Adams, principal of the University of Rhodesia, was appointed director of the LSE. Since Ian Smith's declaration of UDI in 1965 Rhodesia had been, in the eyes of the British government, an illegal regime. Moreover, it was noted that when nine lecturers had been imprisoned without trial in Rhodesia they had received no support from Dr Adams, who had instead agreed with Ian Smith that the nine were 'subversives'. Students at the LSE felt that their college, with its tradition of taking undergraduates from black countries, was not the most suitable home for Walter Adams. David Adelstein, the president of the students' union, wrote a letter to *The Times* saying as much; he was promptly suspended by the college authorities.

In view of the student movement's later associations with the Left, it is noteworthy that at this early stage it was not only socialists who were shocked that a student could be punished for writing to a newspaper. Indeed it was a Conservative student who proposed staging a sit-in, and the students' union overwhelmingly agreed with him. After a ten-day occupation the college agreed to reinstate David Adelstein. Student power had won its first victory.

However, even before the sit-in there had been those who suggested that the argument ought not to be merely about the suspension of a student, nor indeed about whether Dr Walter Adams was a 'good man' or a 'bad man'. In the words of an LSE Socialist Society leaflet of the time, 'the real issue is . . . are we to be content with a situation in which the direction and administration of the LSE is out of the hands of its members and is held to be none of their concern?' On this question the socialists parted company from the Conservative students, most of whom would probably have agreed with the *Sun* newspaper, which asked 'How big a say are students entitled to in the appointment of university staff—if any?' and gave a confident reply: 'none'. The authorities at the LSE concurred: they were prepared to lift David Adelstein's suspension, but they remained steadfast in their conviction that students should not be consulted about the appointment of the college's director.

Although it was only a partial success, the sit-in at the LSE inspired students elsewhere in the country to believe that direct action could work. And it sometimes did, but only as long as the issue was a small and specific one—improving the quality of food in refectories, perhaps, or ending a ban on late-night visitors to student residences.

Students on the Left were dissatisfied with such campaigns. They believed that students should not only devote themselves to improving their own position, which was already a privileged one, at a time when British people were being thrown out of work and Vietnamese people were being bombed by the Americans. A pamphlet put out by left-wing students at the LSE in 1967 carried on its back cover an appeal in support of workers on strike at the Barbican building site in London. 'They have been on strike for six months for the same reason as students at the LSE: the defence of elected representatives and a minimal control over their own situation. Their enemies are intimately linked with ours.'

Advocates of 'widening the struggle' in this fashion were hugely encouraged by the uprising of students and workers in Paris during

Students in revolt: During the demonstrations against the Vietnam war in October 1968, students occupied the London School of Economics to provide sleeping accommodation for marchers. The college authorities retaliated by introducing strict disciplinary rules and putting up gates.

May 1968, when for a brief moment it seemed that another French revolution might be taking place. A new socialist paper, *Black Dwarf*, was set up to celebrate the event; its second issue included an article by the Marxist thinker Ernest Mandel announcing that students were 'the new revolutionary vanguard'. The same sort of hyperbole was evident in the reaction of Tom Fawthrop, an undergraduate at Hull University who visited Paris in May. Two days after his return, while sitting his finals, he ostentatiously tore up his exam papers. 'The issue of examinations,' he declared, 'is also the issue of who shall control education and beyond this the liberation of man.'

Mankind remained unliberated despite Fawthrop's heroic gesture. And many socialist students were uneasy at the thought that they, and not the workers, were supposed to lead the British revolution. As a direct result of the Paris events militant students in Britain formed themselves into a group, the Revolutionary Socialist Students' Federation, whose manifesto committed itself to 'the revolutionary overthrow of capitalism and imperialism' but made it plain that 'the only social class in industrial countries capable of making the revolution is the working class'. Few workers took up the students' offer of unlimited support and solidarity.

While some members of the Revolutionary Socialist Students' Federation were waiting in vain for the workers to 'make the revolution', other students thought it more profitable to prepare for this momentous event in their own universities and colleges. During the massive demonstration in London against the Vietnam war, in October 1968, students occupied the LSE to provide sleeping accommodation for some of the marchers. The college authorities retaliated by installing gates in various parts of the building to prevent future occupations, and by introducing strict new disciplinary rules. The students rose to the challenge, tearing down the new gates, and the authorities duly shut down the LSE. After making a few half-hearted challenges, the students conceded defeat and Robin Blackburn, a young sociology lecturer who had openly sided with the students, was dismissed.

The most successful student protests—as with the original LSE sit-in in 1967—were those in which the participants included people who were not socialists, let alone 'revolutionary' socialists. When students occupied the registry at Warwick University in 1970 they discovered that secret files had been kept on students and staff. Even the most moderate inhabitants of the university found their liberal consciences goaded to outrage by this news; protests ensued. Reviewing the affair ten years later E. P. Thompson, one of the Warwick lecturers who had backed the students, found cause for modest celebration.

> While Warwick University today is very far from the democratic utopia dreamed up by some of us in 1970, it is, I believe, a place governed by rules in which democratic process has some part . . . The moment of encroaching authoritarianism provoked a moment of euphoric libertarian revolt . . . authority was clipped of some powers and placed under more watchful controls.

Was this really all that the student movement of the late 1960s achieved—to enable the democratic process to have 'some part' in the running of a university? It would be easy to draw such a conclusion. By the early 1970s the National Union of Students, which had been run for years by a discredited band of 'moderates', had been taken over by the broad Left; but the character of this new political grouping effectively defused any heady ideas of 'student power'. The NUS's leaders, while issuing militant growls from time to time, took to having friendly chats with government ministers and calling on their members to calm down. One of the more remarkable spectacles of the mid-1970s was the extraordinary chumminess between Sue Slipman, the Communist president of NUS, and Shirley Williams, the decidedly right-wing Labour education minister. The affair reached its inevitable consummation in 1981 when both Sue Slipman and Shirley Williams became founder members of the Social Democratic Party.

However, despite the manifest contrast between the student movement's exaggerated language and the ineffectiveness of most of its actions, one ought not to dismiss it as insignificant. In the late 1960s many students who might otherwise have glided smoothly through university and into a job—without troubling to shift their gaze from lectures, exams and pinball machines—received a crash course in political education. Young people who might earlier have put their trust in Harold Wilson moved away from conventional politics.

Some of them continued doing more or less what they had done as students by organising demonstrations and pickets. Although belief in the efficacy of direct action had not originally been confined to socialists (the successful campaign to stop the South Africans' cricket tour in 1970 had been led by a Young Liberal, Peter Hain), for most of the 1970s it was only the parties of the far Left who persisted in the idea.

Other members of the class of '68 felt less enthusiastic about the all-embracing struggles of the International Socialists or the International Marxist Group. Nevertheless, to use a Sixties phrase, they had had their 'consciousness raised'. They turned their attention to single-issue pressure groups such as Friends of the Earth. This development was partly influenced by America, where congressional lobbying groups were growing at an extraordinary rate. But it was also caused by the fact that hippy ideology—subscribed to by many people who weren't actually hippies—had priorities which were not shared by political parties, whether the Conservatives or the International Socialists. These concerns included pollution, the 'throwaway society' and drug laws. There arose the idea of 'personal politics'—most notably in the women's movement and the campaign for gay rights.

Whether they sought to change the world through attending feminist discussion groups or by standing on picket lines, the veterans of the late 1960s rebellions agreed on one thing: Parliament had nothing useful to say on any of the subjects which they considered important. Their opponents thought so too. Neo-Nazi organisations such as the National Front and the British Movement swelled alarmingly in the 1970s. As far as the House of Commons was concerned, these groups were unimportant; but to black people the threat they posed was real enough. In 1977, as parliamentary indifference continued, the Anti-Nazi League was formed and the rebels of the late 1960s re-emerged to join a new generation, that of the punks.

Two years later, in 1979, the British government agreed to play host to American Cruise missiles. Parliament was not consulted, just as it had not been consulted about the hugely expensive modernisation of Britain's 'independent nuclear deterrent', the Polaris missile. Again, the House of Commons appeared to be ineffective in stopping a serious threat, and once again an alliance was formed between teenagers of the Eighties and rebels of the Sixties, who were joined by veterans of earlier peace marches in the Fifties. The Campaign for Nuclear Disarmament succeeded where conventional politicians had failed, by forcing the danger of nuclear war into the public consciousness. Its new figurehead was E. P. Thompson, a man who managed the impressive trick of being both a CND marcher from the Fifties and a university rebel from the Sixties. The sudden and astonishing rebirth of CND began with an article by Thompson published in the *New Statesman* at Christmas, 1979. Half way through the article, snorting in exasperation, Thompson wrote:

> Politics has nothing left to it now but this: lies, disinformation, the management of opinion, the theatrical show of legitimation. Decisions are taken elsewhere . . . Politicians are the servile and oily-tongued liars, the shady brokers who put these decisions across.

Banning the bomb: In the early 1960s, as in the early 1980s, the Campaign for Nuclear Disarmament succeeded where conventional politics had failed by forcing the dangers of nuclear war into public consciousness and rousing thousands of people. But the bomb was still there.

It would be hard to find a better epitaph for the politics of the Wilson era. It was Wilson, after all, who had wanted defence to be taken out of politics.

SEX

'Sexual intercourse began in 1963' Philip Larkin.
'Is John Peel the sort of person you would be happy to see married to your daughter?' Brian Leary.

In 1936 Edward VIII was forced to abdicate because of his desire to marry a divorced American woman. In 1953 newspapers in the United States and Europe printed rumours that the Queen's sister, Princess Margaret, was also in love with a divorcee, Group Captain Peter Townsend. Reaction in Britain was indignant. The *People*, a mass circulation Sunday paper, announced: 'The story is of course utterly untrue. It is quite unthinkable that a royal princess, third in line of succession to the throne, should even contemplate a marriage with a man who has been through the divorce courts.'

After two years of agonising, on 31 October 1955 the Princess issued a statement to the effect that she would not be marrying Peter Townsend after all, 'mindful of the Church's teaching that Christian marriage is indissoluble'. She was universally applauded. *The Times* declared that 'all the peoples of the Commonwealth will feel gratitude to her for taking the selfless, royal way which, in their hearts, they had expected of her'.

In the view of the popular press (which believed that it spoke for the British working class) and of *The Times* (which gave voice to the attitudes of the Establishment), Victorian morality had been threatened but had emerged thankfully unscathed. But other challenges appeared. Reviewing John Osborne's play *Look Back in Anger* in 1956, Kenneth Tynan wrote that the hero's 'casual promiscuity' was representative of modern youth. In the following three years several other plays appeared which were opposed to conventional sexual mores.

These plays were, of course, seen only by a small number of people, living in London, who might collectively be described as the liberal intelligentsia. But in 1959 a much wider audience was reached, when Jack Clayton's film of the novel *Room at the Top* was released. The main character, Joe Lampton, is a young working-class man in search of sexual and social advancement. After he has made love with a woman on a river bank, she gasps: 'Oh Joe, wasn't it super, wasn't it simply super!' The British public had never before heard sex referred to so unashamedly; nor had they previously heard an admission that sex might be enjoyed by women as well as men. The film was enormously successful in Britain, and even more so in the United States, where it won two Oscars. Its popularity in Britain was particularly remarkable in that the film had been given an X certificate—which had hitherto been thought to mean commercial disaster. Once *Room at the Top* had shown that a film could deal with sex without losing profitability, other film makers were quick to shed their inhibitions.

The *New Yorker* wrote of *Room at the Top* that 'bourgeois morals take an awful drubbing here', while another American critic praised the way in which the film's characters 'commit adultery like recognisable (and not altogether unlikeable) human beings. And the effect is startling.' The film had left the floodgates of repressive morality leaking dangerously, and it was clear that they would collapse altogether if nothing was done. In 1960 the guardians of Britain's morals decided that legal action might stop the flood.

Penguin Books had been founded in 1935 by Allen Lane, a publisher who believed that literature should be sold at a price which ordinary people could afford. He began to issue paperbacks, sold at 6d each. The result was astonishing: by 1960, a quarter of a century after its foundation, Penguin had sold 250 million copies of its books.

In August 1960 Penguin announced its intention of publishing, in full, D. H. Lawrence's novel *Lady Chatterley's Lover*, which had in the past been available only in expurgated form. The Director of Public Prosecutions acted fast, and on 20 October a jury at the Old Bailey began hearing the case of *Regina* v *Penguin Books Ltd*, in which Penguin was accused of 'publishing an obscene article'. The charge was brought under the Obscene Publications Act of 1959, which had, ironically, been introduced in order to prevent serious literature being prosecuted as if it were pornography. In order to prove its case, the Crown therefore had to prove that *Lady Chatterley* was not literature but mere titillatory smut. Yet the case was about far more than this. In effect, sex itself was in the dock.

This was made apparent when Mervyn Griffith-Jones, the prosecuting barrister, gave his opening address to the jury. They had to decide, he said, whether the book would tend to deprave and corrupt. His definition of depravity was broad: 'Does it [the book] suggest to the minds of the young of either sex, or even to persons of more advanced years, thoughts of a most impure and lustful character?' Griffith-Jones assured them that he was not approaching the matter in any 'priggish, mid-Victorian' way, yet most of his arguments suggested otherwise. He explained what he meant by saying that the book promoted impure thoughts: 'It sets upon a pedestal adulterous and promiscuous intercourse. It commends, and indeed it sets out to commend, sensuality as a virtue.' The jury should test the book—'and test it from the most liberal outlook'—by asking themselves the following question: 'Is it a book that you would even wish your wife or your servants to read?'

The nineteenth-century whiff of this question caused laughter in the courtroom. But Griffith-Jones had, unwittingly, revealed the very nature of the prosecution's case. The atmosphere was that of a small and private club whose members fear that the riff-raff may be let in. There was no suggestion that anyone who was actually in court might be depraved or corrupted by *Lady Chatterley*. What irked the Establishment was that people outside—wives, servants, children and the great mass of the British public—might get their hands on the book. The defence summoned several dozen distinguished figures—including the novelist E. M. Forster, Dame Re-

becca West and numerous professors—to testify that they had read the unabridged version of *Lady Chatterley* years before and had not been depraved by it. John Robinson, the Bishop of Woolwich, went so far as to say that 'what Lawrence is trying to do is portray the sex relationship as something essentially sacred . . . as in a real sense an act of holy communion'. By contrast, the prosecution were unable to produce a single witness; they had apparently not found anyone who would admit to being corrupted by the novel.

The fact that the liberal intelligentsia had been so unanimous in their support for *Lady Chatterley* did not surprise or worry the prosecution. University lecturers and literary critics were, like judges and barristers, already members of the club. There need be no fear that *they* would be corrupted by unfettered discussion of sex, or generous use of four-letter words. As the judge put it in his summing up, the true cause for concern was that the novel was to be made available in a cheap paperback and thereby 'put within the grasp of a vast mass of the population'. The judge emphasised the distinction between club members and riff-raff: 'You know, once a book goes into circulation it does not spend its time in the rarefied atmosphere of some academic institution . . . it finds its way into the bookshops and on to bookstalls, at 3s 6d a time, into public libraries, where it is available for all and sundry.'

The jurors failed to accept that people in 'rarefied' institutions should be allowed to read about sex while 'all and sundry' weren't. On the sixth day of the trial, after considering their verdict for three hours, the jury pronounced Penguin Books not guilty.

One of the prosecution's main objections to Lawrence's novel had been that it depicted a woman (Lady Chatterley) finding sexual fulfilment with a man who was not her husband. This was what Griffith-Jones had meant when he referred to the book 'putting adultery on a pedestal'. As we have seen in the case of Princess Margaret and Peter Townsend, the Establishment still presented itself as being uncompromisingly pure: sexual relations should take place only within marriage, and marriage was sacred. And even if the masses were now taking a more relaxed attitude (as was suggested by the success of films such as *Room at the Top*, or by the fact that two million copies of *Lady Chatterley* were sold in the weeks after the trial), members of the ruling class continued to promulgate the myth that their own morals were of unblemished Victorian probity. Many people suspected that it was untrue; and in 1963 they were given the evidence they required, as for months on end Britain was treated to a succession of revelations about the sex lives of the great and the good.

In the spring of 1963 there was a growing number of rumours about a sexual liaison between the minister for war, John Profumo, and a show-girl called Christine Keeler. There had indeed been an affair, but it had been brief and had finished two years earlier, in 1961. Profumo had met Keeler one weekend when he and his wife were staying at Lord Astor's house, Cliveden. Christine was spending the weekend at a cottage on the estate, which her friend Stephen Ward rented from Lord Astor. Having seen her in the swimming pool, Profumo began to press his attentions on her; Christine gave in, although she later said that their sexual relations were 'no more than a handshake'. The security services became alarmed, since Christine was also friendly with a naval attaché from the Soviet embassy, Ivanov, who was almost certainly a KGB agent. Profumo was warned off, and by the end of 1961 his affair with Christine Keeler was over.

Stories of Profumo's behaviour began to circulate early in 1963, but no newspaper dared to print them for fear of the libel laws. Then a Labour MP, George Wigg, referred to the rumours in the House of Commons and demanded a government statement. Profumo obliged the following day: 'There was no impropriety whatsoever in my acquaintance with Miss Keeler.' But the rumours continued, and Profumo came under increasing scrutiny. On 4 June, two and a half months after his original statement, he

wrote a letter of resignation to Harold Macmillan: 'I said there had been no impropriety in this association. To my very deep regret I have to admit that this was not true, and that I misled you.'

For the next few months, scandal followed scandal. The police investigated allegations that Stephen Ward, the man who had introduced Profumo to Christine Keeler, had been running a call-girl ring. Even though there was little evidence to support this claim, Ward was charged with living off immoral earnings. Both Christine Keeler and Ward's lodger, Mandy Rice-Davies, were summoned to give evidence. Mandy Rice-Davies told the court that she had made love with Lord Astor. When one of the barristers pointed out to her that Astor had denied this, Mandy replied: 'Well, he would, wouldn't he?' The line instantly became a popular catch phrase.

Mandy Rice-Davies's claim to have made love to Lord Astor, coupled with the fact that Christine Keeler had met John Profumo on Astor's estate, gave rise to a number of colourful rumours about 'country-house orgies'. To these were added other stories about a party in Bayswater, attended by Keeler, Rice-Davies and Ward, at which a cabinet minister had served a dinner of roast peacock while wearing nothing except a mask and a bow tie. According to one version of the story, the man had also had a card round his neck, which read: 'If my services don't please you, whip me.' Further rumours suggested that another cabinet minister had been caught having oral sex with a prostitute in Richmond Park. Still more rumours mentioned an orgy involving eight high court judges. 'One, perhaps,' groaned Harold Macmillan to a colleague, 'two, conceivably. But eight—I just can't believe it.' Thousands of people did, however, and their suspicions about the sexual antics of the upper class were reinforced by the sensational case going on in Edinburgh at the time, in which the Duke of Argyll was suing his wife for divorce and threatening to name dozens of co-respondents. The judge in the case described the Duchess of Argyll as 'a completely promiscuous woman whose sexual appetite could only be satisfied by a number of men'. The Duchess was alleged to have taken photographs of some of her lovers in the nude. One of the pictures showed a man from the neck downwards; it was announced in court that a cabinet minister had agreed to have his penis examined in order to prove that he was not the 'headless man'. The public furore became even greater when Stephen Ward was convicted at the Old Bailey. Other than a few vague insinuations from the prosecution, no evidence had been produced to show that Ward was a pimp. He committed suicide after the verdict was announced. To many people it seemed that he had been made the scapegoat for other, more important miscreants.

After Profumo's resignation, as the rumours of orgies in high places became more and more exaggerated, Harold Macmillan had commissioned Lord Denning to conduct an exhaustive inquiry into 'rumours affecting the honour and integrity of public life'. Denning heard evidence throughout the summer and although his sessions were held in private they attracted much publicity. At one stage Denning invited the press in to photograph him behind his desk. When the pictures were blown up, they revealed that one of the pieces of paper on the desk was a letter inviting a senior cabinet minister to come and discuss rumours about his sex life.

Denning interviewed more than 150 witnesses, including several prostitutes. One of them specialised in whipping people; when Denning asked her why her clients should wish to have this done to them, 'I told him I supposed it went back to their nannies. But drivers and people like that who don't have nannies don't ask you to whip them.' All this helped to confirm the public's view that members of the Establishment had for years been guilty of rank hypocrisy, taking a high moral tone in public while privately enjoying every sexual variation in the book. Even the innocent became guilty by association. 'Prince Philip And The Profumo Scandal' screamed one front-page headline in the *Daily Mirror*; the implication of the headline was cancelled out by the story beneath it, which said that rumours linking Prince Philip with the Profumo affair were utterly unfounded. At a garden party in his constituency Harold Macmillan posed for a photograph with the young daughter of a constituent. 'Take your hands off that little girl,' he was instructed. 'Don't you wish it was Christine Keeler?' The spirit of the time was captured in *Private Eye* by the cartoonist Timothy

Summer of scandal: At a garden party in 1963 Harold Macmillan posed for a photograph with the small daughter of a constituent. 'Take your hands off that little girl,' said a voice at his side. 'Don't you wish it was Christine Keeler?'

Birdsall, who drew a picture of crowds milling in Trafalgar Square, among whom was one nearly naked woman calling out 'Come ye and stare atte ye breasts of a duchesse', while another invited the masses to 'Come buye my sweete pornographie! Pictures of ye famous lovinge me!' The drawing was entitled 'Britain Gets Wythe Itte, 1963'.

The scandals of 1963 confirmed the arrival of what became known, to its advocates and opponents alike, as the permissive society. But they did not cause it. In his Reith lectures late the previous year, Professor George Carstairs had pointed out that 'the popular morality is now a wasteland. . . A new concept is emerging, of sexual relationships as a source of pleasure.' In March 1963 the Bishop of Woolwich—the same man who had given evidence in defence of *Lady Chatterley's Lover*—received much publicity

for his book *Honest to God*, in which he argued against the traditionally stern attitude of the Christian churches towards sexuality. Three months before Profumo's resignation, *Time* magazine reported:

> On the island where the subject has long been taboo in polite society, sex has exploded into the national consciousness and national headlines. 'Are We Going Sex Crazy?' asks the *Daily Herald*. . . The answers vary but one thing is clear: Britain is being bombarded with a barrage of frankness about sex.

The effect of the Profumo scandal and the Argyll divorce was simply to remove another obstacle to that barrage.

Under its liberal new director-general, Sir Hugh Greene, the

BBC encouraged broadcasters to be much more daring than before. The satire show *That Was The Week That Was* rejoiced in the Profumo affair and the other scandals of 1963, broadcasting innumerable *doubles entendres* and jokes about sex. Not surprisingly, the corporation decided to take the show off for the duration of the 1964 general election campaign; but after the election satire returned to the screen in even greater quantities than before. *Not So Much a Programme, More a Way of Life* was transmitted three nights a week, and caused considerable outrage when it included a sketch in which a Liverpool priest ordered a working-class woman to have more children. The show was brought off in 1965, but satire returned the following year in the form of *BBC3*. This programme won notoriety when Kenneth Tynan appeared on it and became the first person to use on television the word which had caused so much offence to the prosecution in the *Lady Chatterley* case. 'I doubt', he said, as the cameras rolled, 'if there are any rational people to whom the word fuck would be particularly diabolical, revolting or totally forbidden.' Once again, the BBC found itself under attack for its permissiveness.

The television satirists aimed to shock, and they often suc-

Denning is served: Following the Profumo affair Harold Macmillan commissioned Lord Denning to inquire into 'rumours affecting the honour and integrity of public life'. It was a sizeable task; over 150 people were interviewed.

QUEUING AT MIDNIGHT FOR DENNING REPORT ON PROFUMO AFFAIR, SEPTEMBER 1963

'TW3' TEAM. LEFT TO RIGHT (BACK): LANCE PERCIVAL, DAVID KERNAN, DAVE LEE, ROY KINNEAR, KENNETH COPE, WILLIAM RUSHTON (FOREGROUND): DAVID FROST AND MILLICENT MARTIN

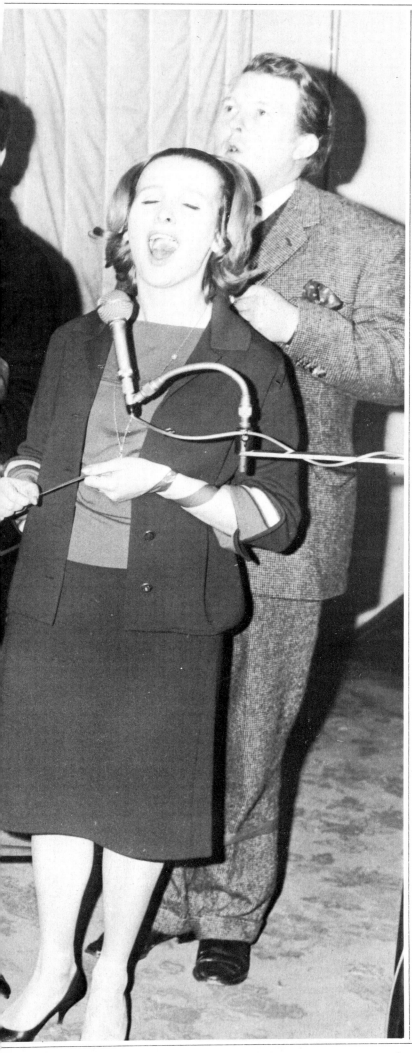

That Was The Week That Was: *The first television satire show was allowed to get way with more* risqué *jokes than previous BBC programmes. It was part of the 'propaganda of disbelief, doubt and dirt' which so infuriated Mary Whitehouse in 1963.*

ceeded. Some critics argued that their 'outrages' were juvenile gestures, carried out in the same spirit as a schoolchild sticking out its tongue at a teacher. Others praised the satire shows for extending the frontiers of what was allowed to be mentioned in public. Reactions to the BBC's other manifestations of permissiveness were equally divided. 'The Wednesday Play', another of Sir Hugh Greene's innovations, sought to present dramatised versions of controversial subjects. One of the plays in this slot, transmitted in the same month in which Tynan used his four-letter word, was *Up The Junction*. It was based on Nell Dunn's account of life among working-class girls in Battersea, south London; one of its scenes was a vivid depiction of a backstreet abortion. Some observers praised the play for its honesty in dealing with the undeniable facts of modern life. Others, such as the *Daily Mail's* television critic, detected baser motives:

> I suggest that at least part of the object of *Up The Junction* was a wish, perhaps an unconscious one, of the Wednesday Play boys to see just how far they could go in a television play with sex and cuss words.

No one denied that many working-class girls were forced to go to backstreet abortionists, since abortion was still illegal in all but exceptional cases. Nor did anyone deny that 'cuss words' were common currency for most of the population. As with the *Lady Chatterley* case, the only question was whether the mass of the population (including 'wives and servants') should be allowed to see and hear these things. Most television producers of the time thought that they probably should—in moderation, of course. As Sir Hugh Greene had said about the satire shows, 'Of course, if we didn't have programmes like *Panorama*, *Tonight* and *Gallery* we would be unjustified in putting on *Not So Much*. But it is a supplement to these other features.' Similarly, in Sir Hugh Greene's view, as long as the BBC continued to transmit hours of 'decent' family viewing there was nothing wrong with slipping in a touch of unwelcome reality now and again.

Even these modest claims were too extreme for some people. In the autumn of 1963 two housewives in the Midlands, Mary Whitehouse and Nora Buckland, drew up a petition against the 'propaganda of disbelief, doubt and dirt' which they believed the BBC was disseminating. 'Illegitimacy and venereal disease are steadily increasing,' they claimed, 'yet the BBC employs people whose ideas and advice pander to the lowest in human nature and accompany this with a stream of suggestive and erotic plays.' The BBC's duty was to 'encourage and sustain faith in God and bring Him back to the heart of our family and national life.' The openly religious message of this appeal might have been thought to be a disadvantage, since all the available evidence suggested that Britain was no longer a Christian country: by the mid-1960s only 5 per cent of the population attended a church service even on Easter Day. However, by hard work Mrs Whitehouse and Mrs Buckland managed to spur much of this 5 per cent into action. They also acquired friends in high places, including backbench MPs and leader writers in the popular press who, although not Christians, felt that the permissive society was something to be viewed with deep suspicion. By the time the Clean Up TV Campaign presented its petition to Parliament in 1965, it had collected over 360,000 signatures.

What Mrs Whitehouse would describe as 'dirt' made up only a tiny fraction of the BBC's output. Most programmes were still traditional, 'decent' fare such as *Come Dancing*, *Dr Finlay's Casebook* or *The Val Doonican Show*. Nevertheless, Mrs Whitehouse's campaign put the BBC on the defensive: Kenneth Adam, the corporation's director of television, organised a conference attended by delegates from fifteen national women's organisations, representing more than ten million women. 'What they had to say about BBC television', Mr Adam declared, 'was very different from what we hear from Mrs Whitehouse.'

By going to such lengths to challenge Mary Whitehouse the BBC unwittingly enhanced her standing, since they were effectively admitting that she was an important and influential figure. Her views began to be listened to with even more respect than before by certain journalists and politicians. In June 1967 the chairman of the BBC, Lord Normanbrook, died suddenly. Harold Wilson appointed as his successor Lord Hill, a former Tory minister who was now running the Independent Television Authority. Dick Crossman's diary gives an account of Wilson's explanation for the appointment: 'Charlie Hill has already cleaned up ITV and he'll do the same to BBC now I'm appointing him chairman.' Mary Whitehouse had triumphed.

When he made Lord Hill chairman, Wilson also increased the number of BBC governors from nine to twelve. There was no doubt that he intended the 'outsiders'—and particularly the chairman—to play a more active part instead of leaving decisions to the professionals such as Sir Hugh Greene and Kenneth Adam. Hill soon showed that he would live up to Wilson's expectations. At the end of 1967 the BBC were due to transmit the Beatles' film *Magical Mystery Tour*, in which one of the songs, 'I am the Walrus', included the line 'Boy you've been a naughty girl, you let your knickers down'. Hill instructed the producers to remove the offending line or cancel the programme. The corporation's staff stood firm, with Sir Hugh Greene pointing out that the song was already being broadcast on the radio without causing any complaint. Faced with this unanswerable point, Hill backed down. But he continued to put pressure on BBC producers. He complained about the use of the word 'bloody' in one play, and the 'excessive' reference to sex in another. Nine months after Lord Hill's arrival Sir Hugh Greene, the director-general, announced that he was retiring early. After his departure the BBC's reluctance to take risks became more apparent. In 1968 one of the BBC's most popular but controversial shows—the comedy series *Till Death Us Do Part*—went off the air indefinitely, with its creators complaining about Lord Hill's new policies. The programme's scriptwriter, Johnny Speight, said: 'We have been irritated by a number of idiotic and unreasonable cuts . . . I would write another series for the BBC but only if this censorship was stopped.' The Clean Up TV campaigners had claimed another victim.

The effect of the sexual revolution on television was, therefore, limited. Young writers and directors were allowed to experiment more than they had in the 1950s, but the authorities were always watchful to ensure that television did not overstep the limits of propriety. This was in marked contrast to the theatre, where censorship was abolished altogether in 1968. Why the difference? Once again, we see the distinction enunciated at the *Lady Chatterley* trial. It was all right for sexuality to be presented to 'rarefied' minorities (such as theatregoers), but exposing the masses to it via television was more of a risk.

In the theatre, the 1960s were thus a time of remarkable freedom. For the first half of the decade the official censor, the Lord Chamberlain, still existed; but his interference was much less effective than in previous decades. When Terence Rattigan wrote his play *Separate Tables* in 1956 he had to change a homosexual scene into a heterosexual scene because the Lord Chamberlain, in Rattigan's words, 'bans any mention of that subject'. But when Joe Orton's first West End play was presented in 1963 the Lord Chamberlain, according to Orton, 'cut all the heterosexual bits and kept in all the homosexual bits'. Orton was exaggerating, since the play, *Entertaining Mr Sloane*, also retained many of its most suggestive heterosexual scenes. The plot involves a young man, Sloane, who attracts the lust of both his landlady and her brother.

Theatricality: 'I myself was nauseated by this endless parade of mental and physical perversion. And to be told that such a disgusting piece of filth now passes for humour ... I hope that the ordinary, decent people will shortly strike back!' Letter in the Daily Telegraph.

Have evening clothes, will travel: James Bond (played by Sean Connery) was the decade's fantasy hero, effortlessly seducing any woman of his choice. His influence spread to advertisements, which soon became full of men in tuxedos and women in bikinis, filmed in exotic locations.

The brother and sister finally come to an agreement whereby they will share Sloane, with each of them having him for six months of the year. Orton preferred to write about sex obliquely rather than directly. This technique enabled him to escape the Lord Chamberlain's blue pen, and also to satirise what he saw as the hypocritical attitude of the middle class towards sex: they were as keen on it as anyone, but their repressive morality forced them to use ludicrous circumlocutions and disingenuousness when discussing it. Typical of this is the seduction method used by Sloane's landlady, who draws attention to the fact that she is wearing nothing under her dress: 'This light is showing me up. I blame it on the manufacturers. They make garments so thin nowadays you'd think they intended to provoke a rape.' Orton's glee in mocking middle-class morality was also evident in his creation of the fictitious figure of 'Edna Welthorpe', a figure like Mary Whitehouse. Under Edna's pseudonym Orton wrote to newspapers and church leaders, calling on them to crack down on those who were undermining decency. After the *Daily Telegraph* had attacked *Entertaining Mr Sloane*, Orton managed to hoax the paper into printing the following letter from Edna:

As a playgoer of forty years may I sincerely agree with Peter Pinnell in his condemnation of *Entertaining Mr Sloane*.

I myself was nauseated by this endless parade of mental and physical perversion. And to be told that such a disgusting piece of filth now passes for humour.

Today's young playwrights take it upon themselves to flaunt their contempt for ordinary decent people. I hope that the ordinary decent people will shortly strike *back*!

The decent people did their best to obey. Theatre impresario Emile Littler and Peter Cadbury, chairman of London's main ticket agency, described *Entertaining Mr Sloane* as 'absolutely filthy'. They also condemned the 'programme of dirt' put on by the Royal Shakespeare Company, particularly Peter Brook's production of the *Marat/Sade*. Protests continued the following year when the Royal Court Theatre staged Edward Bond's play *Saved*, a study of the way in which young people who are rejected by society turn to violence. One critic wrote: 'The scene where a baby in a pram is pelted to death is nauseating. The swagger of the sex jokes is almost worse.' By 1966 Peter Hall, one of Britain's most successful post-war theatre directors, was telling *Time* magazine that 'we are in a theatre that is front-page news. We are denounced as subversive, immoral, filthy—it's all terribly healthy.'

As we have seen, the government felt that theatre did not need close supervision of the type found in television. The Lord Chamberlain himself said that he considered his function outmoded. Following the passage of the Theatres Act 1968, which abolished stage censorship, full-frontal nudity arrived in the West End in shows such as *Hair*, Kenneth Tynan's *Oh! Calcutta!*, and *The Dirtiest Show in Town*. The development had been inevitable; but some liberals found it difficult to accept. The writer A. P. Herbert, who had waged a campaign against censorship in the 1950s, wrote in *The Times* in 1970:

My colleagues and I, in 1954, began a worthy struggle for reasonable liberty for honest writers. I am sorry to think that our efforts seem to have ended in a right to present copulation, veraciously, on the public stage.

A. P. Herbert had touched on an important point. It had been recognised that sex could not be discussed honestly unless one created a liberal climate in which people felt free to talk about such things without risking prosecution. Yet that same liberal climate would, inevitably, also be taken advantage of by those who were interested only in its commercial exploitation. Thus the defence in the *Lady Chatterley* case had not claimed that *no* book should be prosecuted for obscenity; they had merely pleaded for a special exemption for Lawrence because his work counted as 'literature'.

The same tension was visible in the British film industry in the 1960s. Until the 1950s, most 'restricted' films had been given an A certificate, which meant that children under the age of sixteen could attend only if accompanied by an adult. The only films from which children were completely barred were given H certificates—and H stood for horror. The X certificate was introduced in 1951 when it became clear that some films might not be horror movies and yet might still be unsuitable for children because of their references to sexuality. X films became synonymous with titillation.

Room at the Top, as was mentioned earlier, was the first British film to challenge the idea that sex was included in movies only for titillatory purposes. Many others followed, but their quality—and their intentions—varied widely. In John Schlesinger's *Darling*, released in 1963, Julie Christie played a good-time girl in Swinging London who revelled in her promiscuity. The film gave the impression that the Julie Christie character did not find happiness in her frequent bed-swapping, and she was certainly not shown in a particularly attractive light; but no other type of sexual behaviour was espoused either. Perhaps the film was seeking to represent the moral confusion of the time; but to some viewers it seemed to be straightforwardly exploitative, depicting the moral emptiness of Swinging London while also trying to cash in on it. Was it a 'serious' artistic presentation, or was it nothing but a subtle form of titillation? This was the question which the *Lady Chatterley* jurors had been required to answer and, as the 1960s progressed, it was to be asked again and again about films such as *Alfie*, *Georgy Girl* and—most notoriously—Antonioni's *Blow-Up*. Antonioni set out to expose the barrenness of Swinging London, but most critics accused him of actually glorifying the 'desperately unoriginal images of colour-supplement London', a town populated by 'discotheque dollies'. Dollies of a more international kind became one of the essential ingredients of the most extraordinary film success of the 1960s—the series of James Bond films which commenced with the release of *Dr No* in 1962. Bond, played by Sean Connery, was a suave, all-action fantasy hero whose chief distinguishing feature—as with Jimmy Porter in *Look Back in Anger*—was his casual promiscuity.

The characteristic image of the James Bond films—an impossibly attractive man effortlessly seducing gorgeous and sophisticated women—was soon imitated in other media, particularly in advertisements. In the 1950s a firm which wished to advertise a particular brand of shampoo would produce an advertisement which stated simply that its shampoo was good for hair. Products were, generally, advertised on their merits. But in the 1960s, as has already been pointed out in the discussion of Harold Wilson, image often became more important than reality. Thus to advertise a bar of chocolate, bikini-clad women would be filmed walking along a tropical beach, hips swinging alluringly. To advertise bath salts, a woman would be shown luxuriating in the foam while a handsome young man rode up to her house on a white stallion. To advertise cigars or rum, young women would be pictured emerging from the sea with their wet bathing suits clinging to their skin. All these advertisements carried an implicit promise of sexual favours. It is unlikely that many male viewers actually believed that, if they lit up a particular brand of pipe tobacco, women would rush up to them in the street, helplessly seduced by the aroma; nor is it probable that the female audience expected that their new perfumes would have quite such a dramatic effect as was suggested by the advertisements. Nevertheless, these images did succeed in imbuing even the most mundane product with a certain sexual glamour.

Commercial exploitation of the new sexual atmosphere was also evident in the backstreets of large provincial cities and, especially, the London district of Soho. In April 1961 Paul Raymond, owner of the Raymond Revuebar strip club in Soho, was convicted of keeping 'a disorderly house' and fined £5,000. For the purposes of the case 'a disorderly house' was defined as a place which put on performances 'amounting to an outrage of public decency'. Passing sentence, the judge told Raymond:

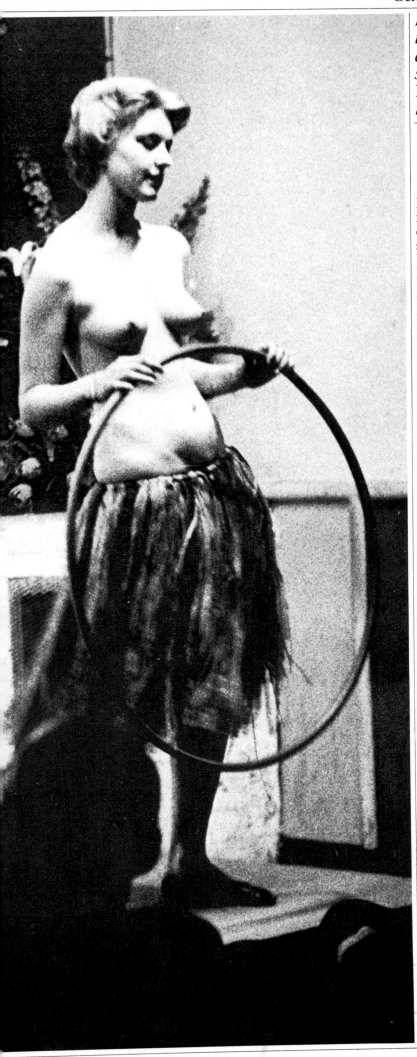

Britain goes topless: 'On a main station bookstall in London recently the display of nudes swamped any other publication — and behind the counter stood, in scanty black corset, the month's Penthouse Pet, *autographing photographs of her naked body.' Lord Longford was unhappy.*

Your establishment and others have been vying with each other to see what degree of disgustingness they can introduce to attract members from all classes who are only too ready, out of curiosity or lust, to see the filth portrayed in this establishment.

But here was the weakness of the judge's case. Many people were indeed 'only too ready' to look at 'filth'; and as long as a market existed there would be no shortage of entrepreneurs prepared to service it. An occasional fine was no deterrent, since the profits to be made from strip clubs and pornographic book shops were huge. Both these types of establishment grew unceasingly in the 1960s.

Pornography was not confined to the streets and alleys of Soho. When it became clear that there was money to be made from nudity tabloid papers such as the *Sun* and the *Daily Mirror* started printing pin-up photographs of semi-naked women accompanied by saucy captions. Even *The Times* accepted a full-page advertisement which featured a nude woman. And the large retail newsagents cheerfully accepted 'soft porn' magazines such as *Playboy* or *Penthouse*. In 1971 Lord Longford set up an unofficial commission of inquiry into pornography, and members of the commission were horrified by what they found:

We imagine that no one who has recently looked round any newsagent's shop or kiosk would dispute the fact that the magazine world has become sex-oriented to an extent that even a few years ago would have seemed unthinkable. On a main station bookstall in London recently the display of nudes swamped any other publication—and behind the counter stood, in scanty black corset, the month's *Penthouse* Pet, autographing erotic photographs of her naked body.

The boom in these magazines was indeed astonishing. By 1970 *Penthouse*, *Mayfair* and *Men Only* each had a circulation of hundreds of thousands; *Penthouse*'s was claimed to be as high as two million. A host of other magazines—with titles such as *Knave*, *Club International*, *Fiesta*, *Heat* and *Open*—sold up to 100,000 copies each. Pornography had become big business. By 1980 the highest paid company executive in Britain was not the chairman of ICI or the managing director of GEC but Victor Lownes, the head of the British end of *Playboy*, whose salary was just under £500,000 per annum. Even more significant, perhaps, was the next highest paid businessman—David Sullivan, a young economics graduate from London University, who had built an empire based on 'hard-core' pornography which was far removed from the jet-set respectability of *Playboy*. Sullivan's magazines specialised in close-ups of women's vaginas ('beaver shots', as they are known in the trade); he also ran a chain of sex shops. Sullivan's salary in 1981 was £325,000 per annum. He, at least, had no complaints about the sexual revolution.

Most producers of sex magazines did not pretend that their aim was anything other than the sexual stimulation of their readers. Some, however, claimed a 'higher' purpose. *Forum*, an offshoot of *Penthouse*, devoted much of its space to articles by sexologists, and readers' letters which were answered by a 'team of thirty-six doctors, therapists, neurologists and others'. The magazine built up a circulation of 200,000 with this mixture; but the Longford commission on pornography was unimpressed:

However sincerely conceived as a beneficial service to those with problems or inadequate sexual knowledge, *Forum* cannot avoid appealing also—we would suggest, largely—to those whose interest is salacious, prurient or fantasist.

Yet again, the *Lady Chatterley* distinction between seriousness and salaciousness was being made.

In June 1970, almost ten years after the *Lady Chatterley* trial, police raided the offices of *Oz* magazine in London and seized copies of *Oz 28*, described on its cover as the 'School Kids' Issue'. Sex and sexuality were about to be put in the dock again.

Oz had been founded in Australia in 1963 by Richard Neville, an undergraduate at the University of New South Wales. The magazine's sixth issue was successfully prosecuted for obscenity; Neville was sentenced to six months' imprisonment, but the verdict was quashed on appeal. In 1966 Neville came to England and resumed publication of *Oz* from his new base in London. The magazine gained a reputation for being bold, funny and often shocking ('obscene and dirty' wrote the *News of the World*, a newspaper which did not usually shy away from publishing dirt). Four-letter words were used freely, and the lay-outs were brash and colourful—so colourful, in fact, that they often made it impossible to read the text of the articles. There had been a number of special issues, including a homosexual *Oz*, a women's liberation *Oz* and a flying saucer *Oz*, each of which was put together by people with a special interest in those subjects and then distributed to what Neville called 'the usual *Oz* readership'—which, by 1970, numbered about 40,000. In its twenty-sixth issue *Oz* advertised for young people between the ages of fourteen and eighteen to come and edit a school kids' *Oz*. As Neville pointed out later, this meant that the paper was to be *produced* by school kids, not aimed at them.

About twenty teenagers helped to compile *Oz* 28. It included a couple of thoughtful articles about rock music, several items complaining about schoolteachers and exams, and a number of articles on drugs. During the *Oz* trial the prosecution gave the impression that the magazine had incited young people to take drugs. In fact, the articles were much more restrained. To take one example, which dealt with medicine and caffeine:

Surely this is what the authorities should be fighting against with a lot more determination and force—these so-called legal drugs that are so much more dangerous than the illegal soft ones? . . . It is time hysteria was overcome and the situation viewed in the correct perspective. I am not trying to advocate the use or legalisation of cannabis. . .

However, although the prosecution was to make much of *Oz*'s references to drug-taking, the main part of the case against *Oz* 28 was its attitude to sex. The central charge against the paper was that it was an 'obscene article' intended to arouse 'lustful and perverted desires' in the minds of young people.

What caused all the fuss? An article by one schoolgirl revealed the not very startling information that some of her classmates had 'decided to wait for the right man' before losing their virginity, while others 'spent weekends fucking in convenient places'. Another article, by a sixteen-year-old called Anne, was a plea for sexual freedom:

This society, although labelled permissive (by society itself), is not free enough to permit man to revert to his natural instincts in public. This ruling does not extend as far as animals. . . One may kiss in certain places but only fuck in a few places at certain times. Surely this idea is as pretentious and puritanical as the old forms of censorship?

Apart from this, the items to which the prosecution took offence were the classified advertisements (which were the one part of the magazine which had not been produced by the teenagers) and a number of the pictures. The front cover of the magazine was a drawing of several lesbian couples embracing. Inside, there was a cartoon of a Medusa who had penises instead of hair sprouting from her head. Most notoriously of all, there was a comic strip in which Rupert Bear, penis erect, raped a naked, reclining granny.

The *Lady Chatterley* case had lasted for six days; the *Oz* trial dragged on for six weeks. In the dock were not the schoolchildren themselves but the three official editors of the magazine—Richard Neville, Jim Anderson and Felix Dennis. With their long hair they looked considerably more out of place in a courtroom than the respectable men from Penguin Books had done in 1960; yet the *Oz* case contained many echoes of its famous predecessor. Once

Schoolkids' Oz: 'This society, although labelled permissive (by society itself), is not free enough to permit man to revert to his natural instincts in public. This ruling does not extend as far as animals,' wrote a 16-year-old girl called Anne, protesting against 'pretentious' ideas.*

again, it seemed that it was not merely the publication which was on trial but all sexual activity except for the missionary position (and even that was acceptable only if carried out within the confines of wedlock). Thus at one stage the prosecuting counsel, Brian Leary, said that the purpose of a particular classified advertisement was 'to glorify the art of fellatio . . . it must have the effect of encouraging people to do that sort of way-out sexual thing'. (A survey conducted in America in 1974 suggested that 72 per cent of people between the ages of eighteen and twenty-one indulged in this 'way-out' act.) Summing up at the end of the trial, Judge Argyle said: 'I wonder how many of *you*, members of the jury, had heard of fellatio before you came into this court.' At one point in the trial the prosecuting counsel suggested that 'pornography is that which places sensuality in an attractive light'—a definition that would put Shakespeare and Goethe, among others, in the dock. In 1960 Mervyn Griffith-Jones had used precisely the same case against *Lady Chatterley*: 'It commends, indeed it sets out to commend, sensuality as a virtue.' As Penguin Books had done in 1960, the *Oz* editors produced numerous expert witnesses to testify to the magazine's moral, literary and artistic worth. Even the 'wives and servants' remark from the *Lady Chatterley* case was echoed when the prosecution barrister, Mr Leary, suggested the jury should disregard the evidence of disc jockey John Peel: 'Is John Peel the sort of person you would be happy to see married to your daughter?'

The *Oz* editors were accused of being obsessive in their attitude towards sex; but the obsession was much more evident in the prosecution case. Leary asked Edward de Bono, one of the defence witnesses, 'What do you suppose is the effect intended to be of equipping Rupert Bear with such a large-sized organ?'

'I don't know enough about bears to know their exact proportions,' de Bono replied.

Leary persisted: 'Mr de Bono, why is Rupert Bear equipped with a large organ?'

'What size do you think would be natural?' was de Bono's reply, at which point the judge told him that he should answer questions and not ask them.

The meaning of the Rupert Bear cartoon continued to elude Leary throughout the trial, even though he had it patiently and eloquently explained to him by Grace Berger, the mother of the boy who had produced the cartoon. 'It was a joke,' Mrs Berger said.

And the joke was this; to put into print what every child knows, that this innocent little bear has sexual organs. Children today are surrounded by, and cannot escape from, the sexual nature of our society: newspapers which are sold by having advertisements based on sex, and which include gossip also based on innuendos about the sexual relationships between people who are not married. This is the world in which our children grow up.

No one would dream of putting advertising agents or the publishers of tabloid papers on trial, charged with corrupting young people. But the editors of *Oz* were young and long-haired. They had little money. They were fair game.

The fact that Neville, Anderson and Dennis were scapegoats became inescapably clear when Leary made his closing speech. He suggested to the jury that reading *Oz* had left an ugly taste in the mouth. 'Let me seek to analyse what that taste was. It's the very epitome, is it not, of the so-called permissive society?' No less a person than Roy Jenkins had said that the permissive society was the civilised society; yet he was not in the dock. It was as if the editors of *Oz* were being held personally responsible for all the public manifestations of sex in the preceding decade. And, after retiring for almost four hours, the jury pronounced them guilty.

Judge Argyle imposed stiff sentences—fifteen months for Neville, twelve months for Anderson, nine months for Dennis—but the three men were released after the appeal court found that the judge had misdirected the jury over the meaning of obscenity.

Explaining the ideology behind *Oz*, Richard Neville once said: 'Sexual repression and political repression were part of the same

tradition . . . the destruction of all inhibition is our aim.' These views were shared by the woman who had edited the special women's liberation issue of *Oz*, Germaine Greer. In 1970, the same year in which the School Kids' Issue appeared, she gave a fuller account of her beliefs—and caught the attention of the world—with the publication of her book *The Female Eunuch*.

Contrary to much popular belief, the women's liberation movement did not begin with Germaine Greer. During the 1960s there was, in the words of American feminist Betty Friedan, 'a strange stirring, a sense of dissatisfaction, a yearning that women suffered'. This dissatisfaction grew when educated young women discovered that they were expected to play a subordinate role even in the radical movements of the late 1960s. (The black leader Stokeley Carmichael said that the only position for women in his campaign

Women's liberation: the image of women in advertising and newspapers 'is based on the same perversions as those embodied in much pornography, but its message is couched in language which the average person does not regard as outrageous; and so he listens'.

was 'prone'.) Moreover, many women were inspired by hippy ideology to take up the idea of personal politics, of 'doing your own thing'. Yet they found that they were obliged to perform their traditional functions of cook and child breeder just as much in a hippy commune as in a semi-detached in Surbiton.

It was not only middle-class women who felt this strange stirring. Discrimination against working-class women was just as intense. In 1963 all 400 employees at the Typhoo Tea works went on unofficial strike because a forewoman had dared to reprimand a workman; discipline, the strikers said, should be enforced only by men. The following year 2,500 men went on strike at a disc brake factory because, in the words of one newspaper report, 'they fear a petticoat takeover at their factory': women had been given 'men's jobs' on two assembly lines. In 1968 women workers at the Ford plant in Dagenham got their revenge, when they went on strike to demand equal pay with the men. As Rose Boland, leader of the strikers, put it: 'Personally I think if a woman does the same type of work as a man, she should be entitled to equal pay.'

By 1968 women's caucuses were forming in Britain, and by 1969 several towns had independent women's liberation groups. In March 1970 the first National Women's Liberation Conference was held in Oxford. In November a hundred feminists smuggled themselves into the Miss World contest at the Albert Hall, and ran down the aisles throwing stink bombs, flour and leaflets, and shouting 'We've been in the Miss World contest all our lives.'

Although the women's liberation movement was not fully developed until the 1970s, its seeds had been planted in the 1960s. The disruption of the Miss World contest was an outpouring of

WOMEN'S LIBERATION RALLY, HYDE PARK, 1971 (PHOTO: BBC HULTON PICTURE LIBRARY)

pent-up frustration at the end of a decade in which women's bodies had been used to sell everything from motorbikes to fertilisers. The permissive society, which was supposed to bring women greater sexual freedom, had in fact meant (according to Germaine Greer) that 'more girls permit more (joyless) liberties than they might have done before'. The Pill had become widely available in Britain in the 1960s, and had been praised for giving women full sexual independence. Yet by the end of the decade some women felt that its introduction had given women more worries (might there be unpleasant side effects?) while relieving men of the need to buy sheaths. And even if sex was more freely available, sexual relations were still based on the same old patterns of dominance that had persisted since time immemorial. In this respect, the influence of advertising and other 'respectable' commercial exploitation of women—such as women's magazines—was believed to be more insidious than the more obvious pornography. As long as female submissiveness was regarded as normal, relations between men and women were bound to be unsatisfactory. As one group of members of the Women's Liberation Workshop put it, the image of women in advertising and newspapers 'is based on the same perversions as those embodied in much pornography, but its message is couched in language which the average person does not regard as outrageous; and so he listens'. For most women, sex was still conducted largely on the terms dictated by men. A woman who challenged this state of affairs—by suggesting, for example, that the simple penetration of the vagina by the penis might not always be the most pleasurable sexual act—risked being dismissed as a lesbian. It was hardly surprising that some women who had previously been exclusively heterosexual began to wonder if lesbianism might not be such a bad idea after all, if it enabled them to escape the male obsession with the vagina.

Sexual politics were not confined to women. During the late 1960s homosexuals, particularly male ones, waged an increasingly vociferous campaign against their persecution by 'straight' society. Lesbianism had never been outlawed in Britain because, according to legend, Queen Victoria had refused to believe that it could exist. But male homosexual behaviour was a criminal offence, for which the penalties were severe. As late as 1963 a 22-year-old labourer and a 24-year-old American airman were sentenced to three years in prison for buggery and indecency.

In 1957 an official inquiry, chaired by Sir John Wolfenden, had recommended that homosexual acts in private should no longer be illegal, although it added that

> the limited modification of the law which we propose should not be interpreted as an indication that the law can be indifferent to other forms of homosexual behaviour, or as a general licence to adult homosexuals to behave as they please.

The following year a group of liberal politicians and academics formed the Homosexual Law Reform Society to campaign discreetly, behind the scenes, for Wolfenden's 'limited modification' to be carried out. Their activities took a long time to achieve results. In 1962 the Labour MP Leo Abse proposed the introduction of a modest bill, but was defeated. Three years later Lord Arran successfully introduced a bill in the Lords which included Wolfenden's proposals, and Humphrey Berkeley produced a similar bill in the House of Commons; but these attempts collapsed when Parliament was dissolved for the general election of 1966. After the election the bill was revived by Lord Arran in the House of Lords and Leo Abse in the Commons; it wound tortuously through its first and second readings and its committee stage before passing into law in July 1967.

The Sexual Offences Act of 1967 was hardly a stupendous triumph. It did not apply to Scotland or Northern Ireland, where

Bodily function: 'Does it suggest to the minds of the young of either sex, or even to persons of more advanced years, thoughts of a most impure and lustful character?' Whatever the answer, 'sex has exploded into the national consciousness', according to one magazine in 1963.

OVERLEAF: YOKO ONO'S FILM OF BOTTOMS, 1967

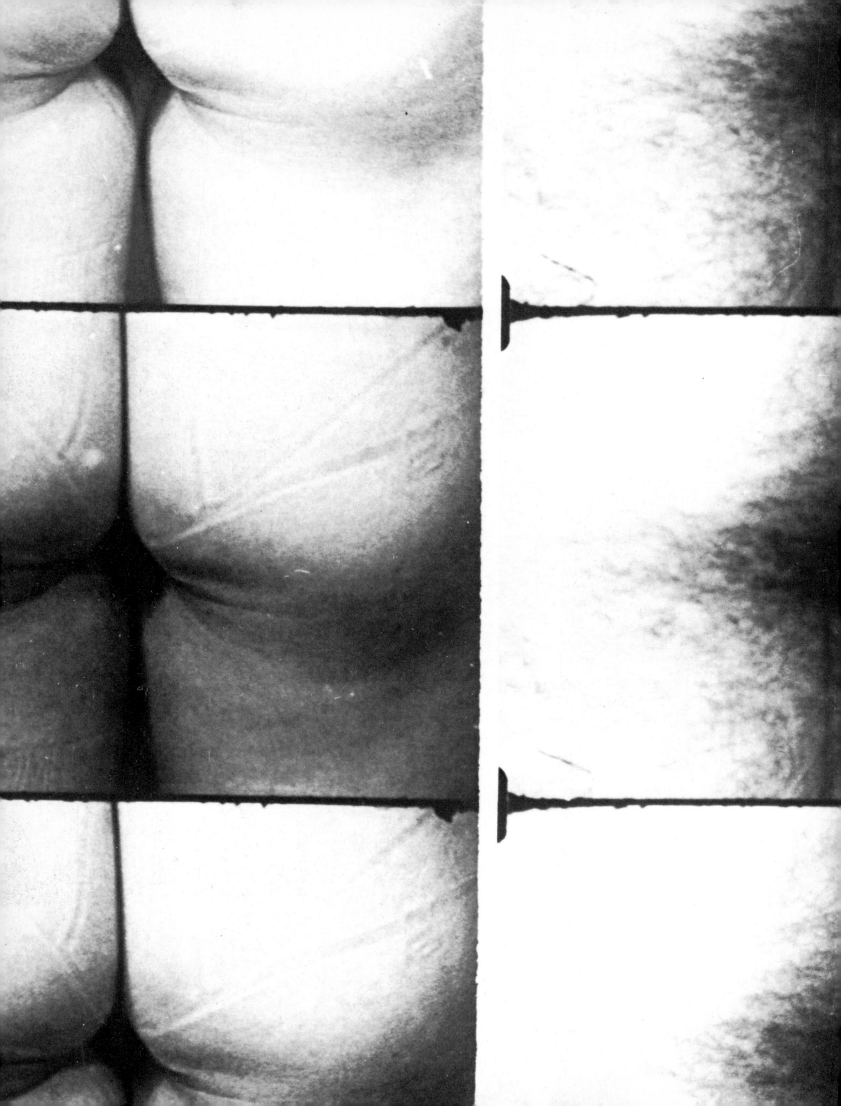

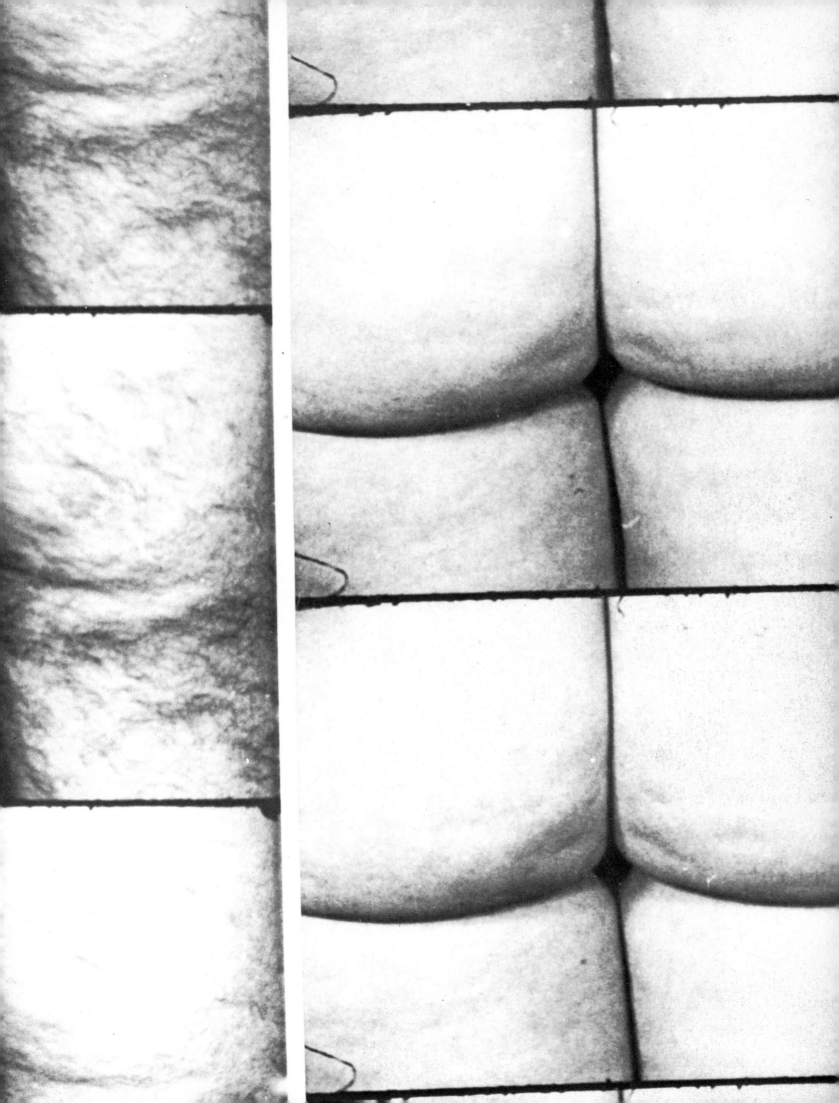

the law was not changed until the 1980s. It also exempted the merchant navy and the armed forces. And the bill embodied a logical contradiction. By legalising certain homosexual acts Parliament had, in theory, accepted the principle that homosexuality was not a dangerous pestilence; yet at the same time, by setting the age of consent at twenty-one while for heterosexuals it was sixteen, Parliament apparently *had* accepted that homosexuality was dangerous. Moreover, homosexual acts between consenting adults over twenty-one were only to be permissible in private, and it soon became clear that the definition of 'private' was to be a strict one. A caravan was not private, for instance; nor was any place where a third person 'might' be present (the implication was that homosexuals always had to lock their bedroom door before making love). In the years following the Act the number of prosecutions of homosexuals actually increased.

Meanwhile, in the United States, an embryo gay liberation movement had begun to emerge from the youth protests of the late 1960s. In 1968 the North American Conference of Homophile Organisations adopted as its slogan the phrase 'Gay is Good'. But the single event that brought the gay movement to life occurred in June 1969 when police raided a gay bar called the Stonewall Inn on Christopher Street, New York. Such raids were common, but what was unprecedented was that on this occasion the gays fought back. Immediately after the Stonewall riot the New York Gay Liberation Front was born; the London Gay Liberation Front was formed a year later. Its first public appearance was in November 1970, when about 150 gays made a torchlight procession across Highbury Fields in North London, to protest against the arrest of a Young Liberal for 'importuning'. Aubrey Walter, one of the founders of the London GLF, later explained the importance of this display:

> I remember this as a very exhilarating moment for homosexuals in Britain, to actually be banded together in public for the first time, holding hands and shouting our 'Give us a G' slogan . . . We kissed warmly and perhaps a little dramatically for the press. We all felt so tremendously high.

Like feminism, gay liberation did not come of age until the 1970s. Its rise had, however, been made possible by the experience of the 1960s. As the press never ceased to point out, a sexual revolution was taking place in Britain. But every step towards sexual liberation was hindered by commercial interests which, in the name of permissiveness, created new forms of sexual guilt to replace the old ones.

The 1960s are often remembered as a period of great parliamentary reforms in the spheres of sex and morality. Considering the supposedly liberal climate of the time, the few measures that did pass through Parliament seem decidedly modest. It is also noteworthy that all of them came from the hard work of a few determined backbenchers, rather than from any special moral initiative by the government; the bill which legalised homosexuality between consenting adults in private was passed in 1967 after years of effort by Leo Abse, Lord Arran and a few others. Two years later, after an equally long campaign, the divorce laws were reformed. Divorce had previously been allowed only if one partner in a marriage had committed a 'matrimonial offence' such as adultery. A 'guilty party' could not sue for divorce; more ludicrously still, divorce was not permitted even when both partners consented to it. As a result, if a married couple wanted a divorce, the husband would have to take himself off to Brighton for the weekend with a prostitute and make sure he was photographed by private detectives while he was in the woman's company. The wife could then apply for a divorce on the grounds of her husband's fictitious 'adultery'.

This was plainly a preposterous state of affairs. By 1966 even the Church of England accepted that divorce ought to be allowed in cases where a marriage had clearly and irretrievably broken down. In 1968 the Labour backbencher Alec Jones, guided by Leo Abse, introduced his Divorce Reform Bill. It passed into law the following year, and in 1970 the Matrimonial Property Act established that, if family property had to be split up because of a divorce, a wife should be entitled to the same share as a husband.

The other reforming piece of legislation in the 1960s was the Abortion Act of 1967, which was introduced by a newly elected young Liberal MP, David Steel. Before Steel's Act, the law forbade all 'unlawful attempts to procure a miscarriage', except where it was necessary to preserve the life of the mother. For some years rich women had been able to obtain abortions in expensive private clinics, while working-class women had to submit themselves to the dangerous and often unscrupulous backstreet abortionists. By the mid-'60s an increasing number of people argued that the existing law was too restrictive. In December 1965 a Church of England working party suggested that abortion could be justified 'in certain circumstances' if there was a risk to the mother's life 'or well-being'. David Steel's Act made abortions legal as long as two doctors were satisfied that it was justifiable, either because of a danger to the physical or mental health of the mother or her existing children, or because there was a substantial risk that the baby might be born seriously handicapped. This reform was too much for some people; in the 1970s the Society for the Protection of the Unborn Child lobbied vigorously for Steel's Act to be tightened.

The effects of the 'permissive society' in the 1960s on people's actual sexual behaviour are hard to quantify since, for obvious reasons, information on people's sex lives is not easy to collect. A survey in 1964 suggested that 16 per cent of young people between the ages of fifteen and nineteen had had some kind of sexual experience; ten years later, another survey found that the figure had gone up to 48 per cent. The trend was to begin sex at an earlier age: in 1964, 6 per cent of boys and 2 per cent of girls had lost their virginity by the time they were fifteen; in 1974 the figures were 26 per cent and 12 per cent respectively. The expansion of higher education, which meant that large numbers of young people were living away from home in the relaxed atmosphere of a student residence, must also have had some influence: a study at Durham University in 1970 found that 93 per cent of female students were virgins when they started their courses, but only 49 per cent were still virgins by the time they graduated. This trend almost certainly became more marked in the 1970s. In 1980, analysing questionnaires filled in by 10,000 of its readers, the magazine *19* found that 26 per cent of them had had some sexual experience before they were sixteen. Only 12 per cent of readers aged twenty or twenty-one claimed still to be virgins. The readership of *19* is not, of course, a representative sample, and in itself it hardly justifies the magazine's claim that 'the virgin bride has become a rarity'. Nevertheless, the findings do confirm the impression that more teenagers than before are sexually experienced, and they are becoming so at a much earlier age. They are also marrying younger: in 1961 there were 136,000 married people in Britain who were aged between fifteen and nineteen; by 1971, the number was 199,000. Perhaps there are still a few virgin brides after all; it is likely that they are working class. Greater sexual freedoms encouraged middle-class women to delay marriage; but for working-class teenagers, living under the parental roof, marriage is often the only way of escaping sexual restrictions.

The consequences of the 'permissive' reform of the divorce laws were striking. In 1965 there were 37,785 divorces in Britain. Ten years later there were 120,552. This change was reflected in the number of one-parent families, which rose from 474,000 in the early 1960s to three quarters of a million in 1976—about 11 per cent of all British families with children. The one thing that remained reasonably steady was the number of babies being born: after reaching a peak of 18.8 births per thousand of the population in 1964, the figure sank back to 16.3 in 1971—the same level as in 1950.

There was one other small indication of the effects of the permissive society. The word 'fuck'—repeated innumerable times in the *Lady Chatterley* case, uttered on television by Kenneth Tynan, and dragged into court again for the *Oz* trial—finally entered the *Oxford English Dictionary* in 1972.

Flaunting it: 'Children today are surrounded by, and cannot escape from, the sexual nature of our society,' said one Oz *witness. 'Are we going sex crazy?' asked one headline in the* Daily Herald.

CLASS

'Are we to say all men are equal except peers?' Alec Douglas-Home, 1963.

When the Conservatives were returned to office at the general election of 1959, Harold Macmillan announced that 'the class war is obsolete'. He then set about forming the most aristocratic government that Britain had seen in years. It included the Duke of Devonshire (Macmillan's nephew), three earls and a marquess. Macmillan's son-in-law, Julian Amery, also became a minister. The aristocratic atmosphere of the period was heightened by the publicity given to the Duchess of Argyll's divorce, and the even greater attention paid to the supposed high jinks on Lord Astor's estate which were revealed at the time of the Profumo affair. The Edwardian tone became even more pronounced in October 1963 when, following Macmillan's illness, a 'magic circle' of Old Etonians appointed the 14th Earl of Home to succeed him as prime minister. 'After half a century of democratic advance,' Harold Wilson complained, 'the whole process has ground to a halt with a fourteenth earl.' Douglas-Home rose to the challenge. 'I suppose Mr Wilson is really, when you come to think of it, the fourteenth Mr Wilson,' he replied. 'Are we to say that all men are equal except peers?'

Harold Macmillan's obituary for the class war had been rather premature. Indeed, even by the time he uttered it there were signs that class attitudes were becoming, if anything, more intense. In 1956 Jimmy Porter had leapt on to the stage of the Royal Court Theatre, in John Osborne's play *Look Back in Anger*, to denounce the 'chinless wonders' of the British ruling class. John Osborne continued the assault the following year in his contribution to *Declaration*, a collection of essays by angry young men (and one woman). 'I can't go on laughing at the idiocies of the people who rule our lives,' he wrote.

> We have been laughing at their gay little madnesses, my dear, at their point-to-points, at the postural slump of the well-off and mentally under-privileged, at their stooping shoulders and strained accents, at their waffling cant, for too long. They are no longer funny, because they are not merely dangerous, they are murderous.

Another contributor to *Declaration*, the film director Lindsay Anderson, argued that Britain was still 'one of the most class-conscious societies in the world, and I see nothing to be gained from the pretence that this is no longer so'.

Declaration was published in 1957. By the mid-'60s some commentators were arguing that Britain had made great progress towards becoming a classless society. As evidence for their claim, they cited the lionising of figures such as David Bailey, Terence Donovan and Brian Duffy (photographers), Michael Caine and Terence Stamp (actors), David Hockney (painter) and Twiggy (model). The Beatles had gone to Buckingham Palace to be given MBEs by the Queen: what could be more classless than that? The angry young men had, it seemed, finally triumphed. The captions

to the photographs in David Bailey's *Box of Pin Ups*, published in 1965, encouraged this view. Lord Snowdon was praised for his 'cosy classlessness' while Michael Caine was 'exactly right for 1965 in his triumphant classlessness'.

It seemed seductive, but there were gaping holes in the argument. Entertainment had always been a profession in which working-class or lower-middle-class people could rise, as had been demonstrated by Noël Coward and Vera Lynn. As the entertainment industry expanded to incorporate television, fashion photography and modelling, it inevitably allowed a few more working-class talents to reach the top.

More important, the success of Michael Caine and others was not a victory for classlessness. If Britain was becoming classless, presumably there would no longer be any need to refer to a person's class of origin. Yet no article on Michael Caine, David Bailey or Twiggy was complete without an emphasis on the fact that they were genuine Cockneys.

The growth in the number of working-class entertainers was largely a matter of supply and demand. For example, in the late Fifties and early Sixties several film directors wanted to present films which would give a more sympathetic picture of working-class life. Lindsay Anderson had argued in 1957 that working-class characters in British films 'are chiefly comic, where they are not villainous'. They made excellent servants, good tradesmen and first-class soldiers. They cracked their funny Cockney jokes or dreamed about the mountains of Wales. They died well, 'often with a last, mumbled message on their lips to the girl they left behind them in the Old Kent Road'. But this was all they were allowed to do. As Anderson pointed out, 'The number of British films that have ever made a genuine try at a story in a popular milieu, with working-class characters all through, can be counted on the fingers of one hand.'

Anderson, together with other directors such as Karel Reisz and Tony Richardson, set out to bludgeon the British film industry into changing its ways. Their success was rapid. In 1957 Anderson had had to advise actors with a regional or Cockney accent to 'lose it quick' if they wanted to become film stars. Only five years later, the *Guardian* was able to write:

> A British film nowadays, if it is to be taken seriously, must set its scene among the more or less rebellious young people of the industrial North or Midlands; it must be tough, realistic, iconoclastic (possibly nihilistic, too) and thoroughly working-class.

In the five years between Anderson's protest and the *Guardian*'s observation, distributors had been forced to abandon their previous belief that films set in a working-class milieu would not attract people to the cinema. *Room at the Top*, released in 1959, had begun the trend. Two years later came the Karel Reisz film *Saturday Night and Sunday Morning*, which earned £100,000 in its

first three weeks on the London circuit. Albert Finney, a grammar-school lad from Salford, played the film's truculent anti-hero Arthur Seaton, a factory worker whose defiant philosophy is 'Don't let the bastards grind you down.' He puts it into practice by drinking and womanising to compensate for the monotony of his job in a bicycle factory.

Albert Finney's origins were lower middle class rather than working class; even so, this was a considerable advance. And in 1962 an unequivocally working-class actor, Tom Courtenay, rose to stardom in *The Loneliness of the Long Distance Runner*. Directors were coming to realise that if they wished to give a realistic picture of working-class life they needed working-class people to play the parts. Courtenay fitted this requirement perfectly: his father had worked as a paint stripper in Hull docks. Nevertheless, Courtenay himself recognised that the success of a few working-class actors and writers did not in itself signify any change in the class system. 'It's simply a release of certain talents from that class,' he told the *Daily Express* in 1961.

Such a release of talents did not imply that class was being abolished. To young members of the upper class such as Lord Snowdon and Kenneth Tynan, the existing culture was etiolated and in need of invigoration from below, just as interbred families cannot survive without sometimes accepting new blood from outside. The attractiveness of figures as diverse as the Kray brothers and Michael Caine was their 'vitality', rejuvenating a worn-out Establishment. Newspapers often pointed out that the appeal of the Beatles transcended class, but barriers between the

Smile of success: The 1960s saw the rise of the 'new aristocracy' — professions such as photography and modelling, which had suddenly become fashionable and highly remunerative and, most importantly, open to East Enders. They were lionised by the old aristocracy.

classes were not demolished simply because 'Twist and Shout' was bought by children at public schools and working-class teenagers alike. The only exciting music of the time was being produced by people who were working class, and so it was inevitable that young aristocrats would embrace the Beatles.

This development had been foreseen almost exactly a hundred years earlier by none other than Karl Marx, who had used the following analogy in *Das Kapital*:

The circumstance that the Catholic Church in the middle ages formed its hierarchy out of the best brains in the land, regardless of their estate, birth or fortune, was one of the principal means of consolidating ecclesiastical rule and suppressing the laity. The more a ruling class is able to assimilate the foremost minds of a ruled class, the more stable and dangerous becomes its rule.

One does not have to be a Marxist to notice that the assimilation of the foremost talents of the 'ruled class' was one of the characteristics of the 1960s; and of course it did not apply merely to Paul

DAVID BAILEY AND CATHERINE DENEUVE MARRY EIGHT WEEKS AFTER FIRST MEETING, 1965

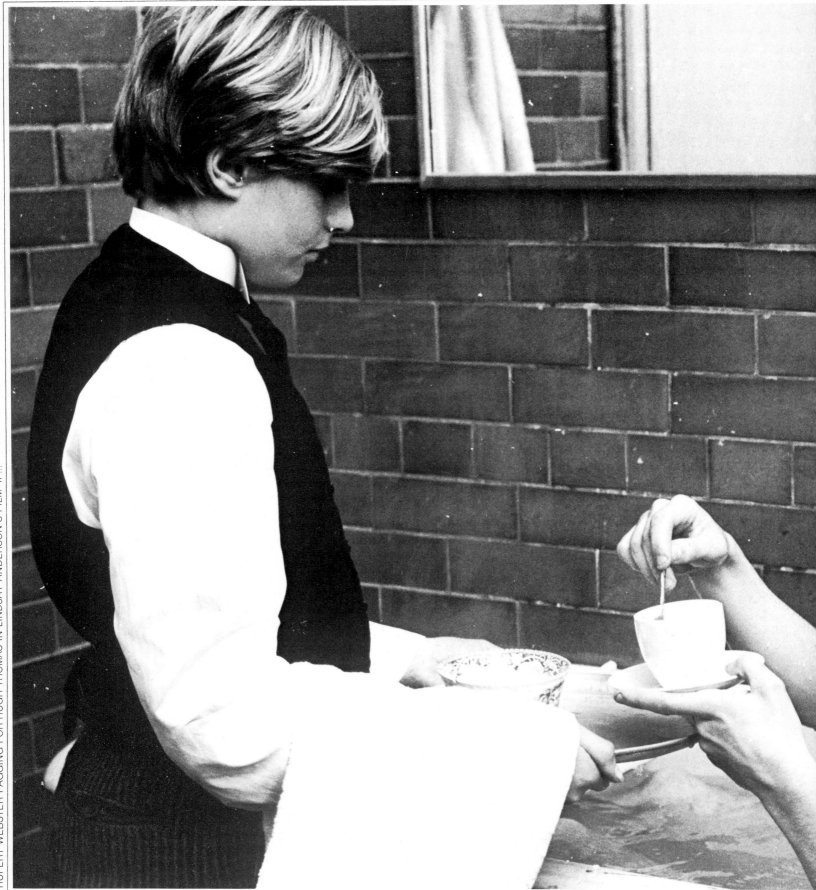

RUPERT WEBSTER FAGGING FOR HUGH THOMAS IN LINDSAY ANDERSON'S FILM 'IF...'

McCartney or John Osborne. Both Conservatives and socialists would agree that British capitalism moved into a more advanced phase in the 1960s. The old, straightforward division between manual workers in industry and the people who actually owned industries was no longer applicable in an age of increased automation and swelling bureaucracy, which created the need for a large class of managers and technocrats. The official reaction to this requirement was the expansion of secondary education after Rab Butler's 1944 Act and the growth of higher education which followed the Robbins report in 1963. Harold Wilson and Ted Heath were thus more appropriate symbols of class mobility in the 1960s than Twiggy or Michael Caine, since most youngsters who 'bettered themselves' did so, like Wilson and Heath, as a result of education. Wilson and Heath were also representative in that they came from the lower middle class rather than the working class.

Harold Wilson's mother was a teacher; his father was an industrial chemist. Both parents were highly ambitious for their son. His father, Herbert, was particularly determined that Harold should go to university; Herbert had himself been denied a university career because his family could not afford to pay his fees.

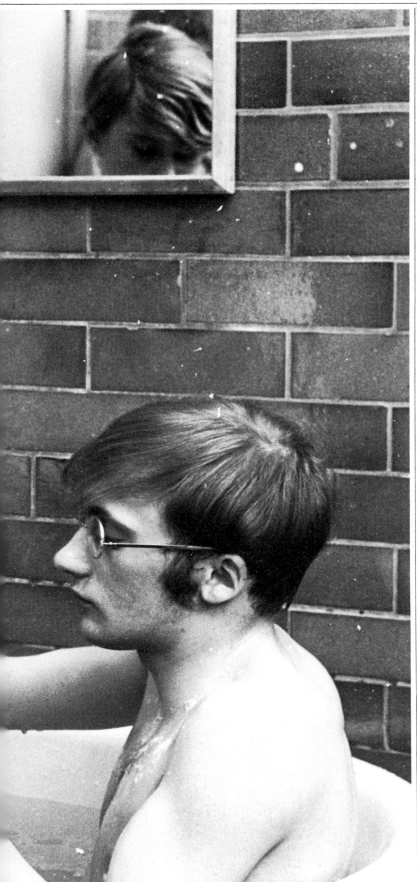

OVERLEAF: HAROLD WILSON IN HIS CONSTITUENCY, 1966

Screen gems: 'A British film nowadays, if it is to be taken seriously, must set its scene among the more or less rebellious young people of the industrial North or Midlands; it must be tough, realistic ... and thoroughly working class.' And so must its actors, of course.

Following the outbreak of war, Beveridge was summoned to Whitehall to chair the government's Manpower Requirements Committee; he took Wilson with him as his secretary. When Beveridge moved to the ministry of labour at the end of 1940 Wilson again went with him, becoming head of the ministry's manpower statistics branch at the age of twenty-four. The civil service, like Oxford, was dazzled by Wilson's prodigious capacity for hard work. In 1942 he was made director of economics and statistics at the ministry of fuel and power. Had he not decided to stand for Parliament in 1945 there seems little doubt that Wilson would have reached a very senior position in Whitehall. But if he had not been able to go to university, it is unlikely that he would have had the chance to show the civil service his talents. Moreover, his work during the war gave him experience of Whitehall and Westminster which proved highly useful when he began his climb up the greasy pole of politics.

In 1965, a year after the election of the Wilson government, Edward Heath became leader of the Conservative Party. His mother had been a domestic servant to a middle-class family. His father had begun his working life as a carpenter, but after the First World War he took a job with a builder in Kent; he was paid well, and in 1930 he used his earnings to start his own building and decorating business. Ted Heath's parents, like Wilson's, were ambitious for their son. He won a scholarship to a local grammar school and was then awarded the organ scholarship at Balliol College, Oxford. Like Wilson, he consolidated his social advance during the war; but whereas Wilson had spent the war years in Whitehall, Heath saw active service and reached the rank of lieutenant-colonel in the artillery. He had become an officer and a gentleman. In 1950 he was elected as a Conservative MP; one of Heath's biographers, Andrew Roth, has noted that the 1950 intake in the Commons 'was exceptional in the large proportion of its new Tory entrants who were ex-officers . . . and [who] had made their way without benefit of family wealth'. With Heath, as with Wilson, there is no doubt that his place at Oxford was the single most important advantage which enabled him to rise from the lower middle class at such speed.

The importance of education to social mobility was confirmed by studies carried out at Nuffield College, Oxford, in the 1970s. For example, a legal executive whose father had been a sheet-steel worker told the Nuffield researchers: 'Without doubt, the main reason [for my higher-level work and living standards] is that I have had the opportunity to go to a grammar school and carry on with further education after I left school . . .'

However, while some people undoubtedly benefited from employers' increasing emphasis on the need for educational qualifications, others found themselves at more of a disadvantage than before. An article in the *Sociological Review* in the mid-'60s pointed out that 'for those who leave non-selective schools at the age of 15 for a manual occupation, this kind of work is becoming more than ever before a life sentence'. This was because the same factors that enabled some working-class children to escape from the type of job that their parents had done—technological progress, specialisation and the importance of formal qualifications—at the same time reduced the possibility of 'working up from the bottom', which was how working-class children had previously bettered themselves. (William Haley, for instance, had left school at the age of fourteen to become a wireless operator; by the 1950s he was editor of *The Times*.) After the introduction of the 1944 Education Act children at state schools were divided by the 'eleven plus' exam: the ones who did well went on to grammar schools, while the rest were sent to secondary moderns. Moreover, within those schools children were placed in different 'streams' according to their academic success—which was measured by their ability to pass exams at the age of eleven. The 'bright' children were

Harold worked hard and invariably came top of his class at grammar school. In 1933 he won an exhibition to Jesus College, Oxford. Wilson was conscious of his good fortune in being at Oxford and he threw himself into his studies to ensure that the privilege was not wasted, often working twelve hours a day. In 1937 he won one of the best first-class degrees that the university had ever seen. He was given a lectureship in economics at New College, thereby becoming the youngest Oxford don for 400 years. In 1938 he was appointed research assistant to Sir William Beveridge, master of University College.

encouraged to take O-levels and A-levels, and to set their sights on university, but the others received an education which concentrated on practical skills at the expense of academic achievement. There would have been nothing wrong with that, of course, had it not been for the increased necessity for academic success if one wished to pursue a career. In effect, then, children's social opportunities were being fixed when they were just eleven years old.

Those youngsters who were condemned to a 'life sentence' of manual labour did enjoy a rather different lifestyle from their parents. Full employment and pressure from trades unions had led to a rise in earnings and a reduction in the length of the working week. Many working-class people were thus able to emulate the middle class in buying cars, washing machines and television sets. This caused some observers to argue that the working class was becoming 'bourgeois'.

But class barriers are not constructed merely on differences in spending power. Workers might be more affluent, but they were still indisputably working class. A survey of more than 400 manufacturing firms in 1968 showed that managerial and clerical staff still enjoyed much greater privileges than manual workers. Managers and office workers were seldom penalised if they did not work a full day; but manual workers still had to 'clock in' on their arrival each day, and had their pay docked if they were late. Manual workers had much less choice about when they could take their holidays; they were less secure in their employment; and their pensions and sick pay were worse than for clerks and managers. Moreover, manual workers still had little incentive to feel involved in their jobs. A man at Ford's car factory in Dagenham described his attitude to his work:

> It's got no really good points. It's just convenient. It's got no interest. You couldn't take the job home. There's nothing to take. You just forget it . . . It's different for them in the office. They're *part* of Ford's. We're not, we're just working here, we're numbers.

For all their affluence, manual workers were no nearer to middle-class job satisfaction. Nor were they able to mix more freely with

members of other classes: middle-class people might chat to working-class people at work or in the supermarket, but they were unlikely to invite them into their homes. Margaret Stacey's study of the social structure of Banbury, published in 1960, revealed the subtleties of the techniques of 'social acceptance'. It was not enough to have a good income; one needed to possess the right 'manners and attitudes'. Moreover, 'you must know or learn the language and the current private "passwords" of the group'. These defensive mechanisms, by which members of one class shield themselves from members of another, are difficult to penetrate.

The most striking consequence of a decade which supposedly made Britain a more classless society was that class distinctions were as persistent as ever. People who bettered themselves through education usually learned the private passwords and adopted the manners and attitudes of the class into which they had moved. The transition was not always entirely smooth. As he moved into grander circles Ted Heath acquired a strangulated parody of an upper-class accent. His successor as Tory leader, Margaret Thatcher, was another product of the lower middle class

Street life: 'The school I went to in the North,' Harold Wilson said, 'was a school where more than half the children in my class never had any boots or shoes on their feet.' He later explained that he did not mean that they had gone barefoot — they had worn clogs.

who had risen through grammar school and Oxford University; she went to the trouble of taking elocution lessons.

Both Heath and Thatcher seemed to bear out Richard Hoggart's suggestion, in his book *The Uses of Literacy*, that scholarship children from the working class or lower middle class retained 'an underlying sense of unease' when they became 'emotionally up-rooted from their class'. This insecurity was also apparent in Harold Wilson; but whereas Heath and Thatcher showed it by taking exaggerated care to acquire the characteristics of the upper middle class, Wilson's unease manifested itself in his equally exaggerated efforts to show that he was still a working-class lad at

THE OLD SALT MARKET IN GLASGOW

DICK CROSSMAN AT LABOUR PARTY CONFERENCE, 1965

heart. We have already seen how he smoked a pipe in public while preferring cigars in private, and how he devoured HP Sauce and made a point of being photographed with the cast of *Coronation Street* (the embodiment of working-class entertainment) and the English football team. There was also an odd incident early in Wilson's ministerial career, when he told the House of Commons that 'the school I went to in the north was a school where more than half the children in my class never had any boots or shoes to their feet'. A former teacher of his promptly issued an angry denial that Wilson or his schoolmates had ever gone barefoot. Wilson had to apologise; he added that what he had meant to say was that half the children in his class wore clogs rather than shoes. He had accidentally omitted the reference to clogs from his speech, thus giving the clear impression that his schoolmates had no footwear at all.

As a socialist, Wilson naturally liked to emphasise that though he had attained high office he had not lost the attitudes of his class of origin. Class anxieties of a different kind worried socialists from an upper-middle-class background. Dick Crossman, one of Wilson's ministers in the 1960s, was an Old Wykehamist, the son of a High Court judge who had insisted that his family wear evening dress for dinner every day. Crossman himself lived in some splendour at Prescote Manor in Oxfordshire. Early in 1967 he wrote in his diary:

Anne [his wife] and I have a facility of freedom and an amplitude of life here which cuts us off from the vast mass of people and in particular from ordinary people in Coventry [his constituency]. I am remote from Coventry now. I feel it and they feel it too.

Crossman, being a socialist, was troubled by the thought that he might be cut off from the working class. Middle-class people who did not share his political views had no such qualms—indeed, their greatest desire was to see class barriers strengthened. In 1954 the

Public school socialists: The Labour government of 1964-70 was presided over by Harold Wilson, a connoisseur of HP Sauce, but it also included men such as Dick Crossman, Anthony Wedgwood Benn and Lord Longford, who enjoyed 'an amplitude of life'.

SIXTH-FORMERS IN SUSSEX PROTEST AGAINST AMERICA'S ATTITUDE TO CUBA, 1962

middle-class residents of a private housing estate in Oxford put up brick walls across two roads to stop working-class tenants from a nearby council estate walking through the middle-class area on their way to the shops. The walls were demolished in 1959. It seemed an appropriate gesture with which to usher in the decade of classlessness. But such an interpretation would be sadly misleading. The middle-class residents used every means at their disposal—including legal action—to try to prevent the city council from knocking down these remarkable physical manifestations of class hostility. And although the walls disappeared, the attitudes they symbolised did not. As Arthur Koestler complained in 1963, 'in this oldest of all democracies class relations have become more bitter . . . than in De Gaulle's France and Adenauer's Germany'.

There was no let-up in that bitterness in Britain during the 1960s. The new affluence of the working class seems, if anything, to have increased the antagonism felt by some parts of the middle class towards them. Certainly by the early '70s the middle class was more outspoken in its feelings. For their book *Voices From the Middle Class* Jane Deverson and Katherine Lindsay interviewed people in two London suburbs. 'We struggle to buy our own homes and send our children to good schools,' one couple moaned, 'while the poorer people live in council estates and have everything done for them.' One resident, pointing at the council estate, said 'it's the enemy over there!' Perhaps the most extraordinary outpouring of class hatred came from a woman who 'couldn't understand' why anyone should feel guilty about the working class:

We would always be richer in our minds than the working classes, just by reading books. Labourers can earn a lot of money these days. God, they must have money, the prices they charge! But all they are concerned with is revenge, in the petty ways of their minds. Jealousy and bitching is their main occupation.

By the late Sixties and early Seventies many middle-class people had apparently convinced themselves that the higher living standards of the working class had been achieved at their expense. They were not deterred by the fact that there was no evidence for this proposition (middle-class incomes had risen too). They believed it, and used it as a justification for their dislike of the working class. John Gorst MP founded the Middle Class Association, whose admirably vague objective was 'to take whatever action may be deemed necessary to further the interests of members'. Patrick Hutber, a columnist on the *Sunday Telegraph*, invited middle-class readers to write to him with their grievances; he found himself deluged with mail. Hutber's own views were clear enough: he considered the middle class to be 'more adult' than the working class. This was because the characteristic middle-class virtue was thrift—a willingness to postpone gratification—while the working class was incapable of earning money without spending it straight away, unless it was 'saving up' for a specific purpose such as 'a holiday, a colour television set or an expensive coat'. Thanks to the availability of hire purchase, however, the working class were more likely to buy the television set immediately and pay for it afterwards, in instalments.

Here we see middle-class fantasies in all their glory. The 'live now, pay later' attitude for which Hutber criticised the working class was, by the 1960s, equally characteristic of the 'more adult' middle class. (After all, what else does a mortgage represent?) The middle class had long since dispensed with any notions of thrift, and in the 1960s they were just as eager as the working class to fill their houses with electric food mixers, washing machines and stereo systems. What they seemed to resent was the discovery that some working-class people could afford these gadgets too. One of Hutber's correspondents found himself tempted to advocate 'punishments of a primeval character' against the workers.

Nevertheless, the middle class continued to seek excuses for their violent desires by trying to prove that they really had been impoverished by the working class. One of Hutber's readers described himself as being 'up against the wall' on the grounds that he could no longer afford a gardener: 'It amounts to a social revolution.' A persistent middle-class complaint was that 'punitive taxation' had taken money away from them and given it to the

The Duke wore jeans: Woburn Abbey in Bedfordshire, stately home of the Duke and Duchess of Bedford, was the unlikely scene of several 'love-ins'. By the end of the 1960s no aristocratic family was complete without a son or daughter who had 'dropped out'.

working class; but this claim was contradicted by the factual evidence. In 1960 the higher-paid half of the British population, which included most members of the middle class, earned 69.8 per cent of the total personal income; by 1970 the equivalent figure was 69.6 per cent, hardly indicative of a sudden redistribution of wealth away from the middle class.

In spite of figures such as these, the middle class's belief that it had lost ground in the 1960s remained strong. J. B. Priestley, writing as 'an unrepentant bourgeois', protested against the relentless 'egalitarian drive' which 'increases the pressures, already very severe, on our middle class'. In fact, the egalitarian drive had been more than matched by the middle class's determination that class divisions should stay as they always had been. A classification in 1966 suggested that 68 per cent of the British population were working class and 32 per cent were middle class or upper class. A similar exercise in 1975 gave totals of 64 per cent and 36 per cent. Allowing for differences in the sampling method, there had not been any marked alteration in the class composition of Britain. Nor had there been any dramatic change in the advantages enjoyed by people of higher class: at the beginning of the 1960s, a quarter of undergraduates at British universities were the children of manual workers; in 1970 their number had risen by just 3 per cent. By 1971 the chances of public-school children going to university were still more than five times greater than those of children at state schools.

Sir Alec Douglas-Home's Cabinet in 1963 contained only two ministers who had not been educated at public schools. Given Sir Alec's own aristocratic origins this was, perhaps, not surprising. However, the arrival of the 'classless' Edward Heath made little difference: in his 1970 cabinet there were still only four ministers who had been educated at state schools. This extremely slight progress was reversed altogether when Heath was replaced by Margaret Thatcher, the grocer's daughter from Grantham, who made great play of her meritocratic image. In 1979 the Conservative Cabinet included just two people who had not been to public school—and one of them was the prime minister herself.

One member of the working class who did succeed in the 1960s, John Lennon, gave his verdict on the decade in an interview with *Rolling Stone* magazine in 1970:

The people who are in control and in power and the class system and the whole bullshit bourgeois scene is exactly the same except that there is a lot of middle-class kids with long hair walking around London in trendy clothes.

He was overstating the case, perhaps, but not by much. Another person who had noticeably improved his social status in the 1960s, Albert Finney, echoed Lennon's sentiments: 'There is the illusion', he told an interviewer, 'that, because some of us achieved success and affluence, things may be a bit better—but the change is not nearly big enough.'

The system of social apartheid separating one class from another survived the 1960s relatively unscathed. Cinema and television began to portray working-class life, but they did not show people of different classes treating one another as social equals. In fact the cinema provides one of the best examples of the resilience of class attitudes. A popular film of 1959 was *I'm All Right Jack*, in which a factory dispute was presented as a microcosm of British life. The managers were shown to be cynical and corrupt while the workers were callous and bloody-minded. In 1982 Lindsay Anderson released his film *Britannia Hospital*, which also used a labour dispute as a miniature version of Britain. The rulers were cynical and corrupt; the ruled were callous and bloody-minded. In 1959 Harold Macmillan had written off the class war as 'obsolete'. Twenty-three years later it still appeared to be in remarkably fine fettle.

MONEY

'There are people today amassing stupendous fortunes' Sunday Times, 1964.

Revealing an unexpected interest in the philosophy of existentialism, Harold Wilson once said that in the 1960s 'the verb to have has come to mean more than the verb to be'. It is certainly true that hardly a month passed without one newspaper or another lovingly reporting a rags-to-riches tale. One year ago, the story went, this young person was just another backstreet kid; now, he or she has made a million pounds and is an honoured guest at all the most exciting parties in town. Night after night, television advertisements drove home the message: money *does* buy happiness.

In an atmosphere such as this, it was scarcely surprising that gambling was one of Britain's fastest growing industries in the 1960s. It offered the chance of instant wealth: if you thought it unlikely that you would be 'discovered' as the next Tommy Steele, you could always dream of a 100 to 1 winner at Epsom. The government encouraged these dreams: in 1956 it introduced premium bonds, the first public lottery in Britain for 200 years. The bonds were, by conventional standards, an outstandingly bad investment, yet people rushed to hand over their money in the hope that they might win the top prize of £5,000. (When Labour came to office this was increased to £25,000.)

Four years after creating premium bonds, Harold Macmillan's government went even further. The Betting and Gaming Act of 1960 legalised casinos, bingo and off-course betting on horses and dogs. In the following five years the amount of money spent on gambling quadrupled. Soon after the passing of the Act betting shops began to appear in high streets; by 1968 there were 15,782 of them. By the 1970s, a Home Office survey classified no fewer than 20 per cent of British adults as 'regular gamblers', all seeking the elusive wager which would make them rich.

Propaganda emphasising the glamour of sudden wealth was relentless. One of the more remarkable publications of 1965 was *A Box of Pin Ups*, a collection of photographs by David Bailey with captions written by Francis Wyndham. 'David Bailey has photographed the people who in England today seem glamorous to him,' explained the blurb. What united these people was that they had 'gone all out for the immediate reward of success: quick fame, quick money'. They were a strange assortment, representing what was known as the 'new aristocracy'—professions which had suddenly become fashionable and highly remunerative. The subjects of Bailey's portraits included fellow photographers, designers, hairdressers, models, pop groups and advertising agents.

The old Establishment was fascinated by the new tycoons. Asset stripper Jim Slater and property developer Nigel Broackes were invited to dinner by Ted Heath, leader of the Conservative Party. When Mick Jagger was given a conditional discharge for a drugs offence in August 1967, he was flown by helicopter to a secret rendezvous where he was interviewed by, among others, the editor of *The Times*, the Bishop of Woolwich and Malcolm Muggeridge. Even more extraordinary was the breakfast given by David Frost at the Connaught Hotel in London on 7 January 1966. Frost was only

twenty-six years old at the time, but already he was earning £40,000 a year. The invitation to eat bacon and eggs with him proved irresistible to Harold Wilson, the Bishop of Woolwich (again), the Methodist leader Lord Soper, the philosopher A. J. Ayer, and newspaper executives such as Cecil King of the *Mirror* and David Astor of *The Times* and the *Observer*. The only person who declined to come was Paul McCartney.

To qualify for membership of the new aristocracy one had to be rich, and preferably working class. Whether those riches had been obtained by fair means or foul was of rather less importance. Indeed, a few skeletons in the cupboard could be a positive asset. For instance, among the stars of David Bailey's *Box of Pin Ups* were the East End gangsters Ronnie and Reggie Kray: Francis Wyndham's caption to their photograph revealed that 'to be with them is to enter the atmosphere (laconic, lavish, dangerous) of an early Bogart movie'. In smart Soho nightclubs the Krays mingled with politicians and princesses, who were careful not to inquire too closely into how the twins came to have so much money. When the brothers were finally brought to court, in 1969, it was revealed that their empire had been based on violence, extortion and blackmail. In March 1966 Ronnie had shot and killed a man in an East End pub who had called him a 'fat poof'. Soon afterwards a small-time gambler who had criticised the Krays was brutally stabbed to death by Reggie, cheered on by Ronnie's shouts of 'kill him, Reg, kill him'. These and other atrocities earned the twins life imprisonment; those who had previously lionised them fell strangely silent, but expressed no contrition for their part in building up the Krays' confidence. The same happened when the other main London gangsters of the time, the Richardson brothers, were brought to justice. Like the Krays, they had been fawned upon by the *habitués* of West End nightclubs; one Conservative MP had told Charlie Richardson that he ought to go into politics. When the Richardsons appeared at the Old Bailey in 1967 it transpired that their methods had been as gruesome as those of the Krays, if not more so. Anyone who was thought to be 'getting in the way' of the Richardsons' racketeering was coshed or stabbed; some then had electric shocks applied to their genitals, while others had their teeth pulled out with electric pliers.

Until the facts were exposed, however, these gangs were considered just as glamorous as any other people who had, in Francis Wyndham's words, 'gone all out for quick money'. In some cases violence was not even a handicap, as long as it was not as deliberate and horrifying as that of the Krays or Richardsons. In the early hours of 8 August 1963 a group of armed robbers stopped the Glasgow-to-London mail train at Sears Crossing in Buckinghamshire. Their haul was well over £2 million. In the course of the hold-up Jack Mills, the train's driver, was hit over the head and seriously injured; a disagreeable fact that was largely ignored by the press and public. (It was only towards the end of that decade that, in a twinge of conscience, a fund was set up to help driver Mills, by

which time it was almost too late: he died soon afterwards.) What caught the public imagination was the huge amount of money involved. The idea that one could become £2 million richer overnight had the same glamour as David Bailey's new aristocrats. It was in keeping with the spirit of the time and, perhaps inevitably, the great train robbers (note the 'great') acquired the status of folk heroes. The students' union at Southampton University voted to award honorary life membership to Bruce Reynolds, leader of the robbers. This applause was echoed abroad. An Australian newspaper, the *Sydney Daily Telegraph*, wrote in an editorial:

> It proves that the homeland of Dick Turpin and Charlie Peace is not decadent. Britons may not admit they are proud, but in private many are thinking 'For they are jolly good felons' . . . The shade of Jesse James, whose first and most famous score came to a measly 3,000 dollars on a Rock Island Railroad hold-up, would undoubtedly hail his British cousins with a courtly bow and a sweep of his broad-brimmed hat.

Instant money, instant success: the theme was repeated constantly during the 1960s. The notion of earning a reputation and a fortune over a period of years was thoroughly old hat. As Kitty Muggeridge said of David Frost, 'he rose without trace'.

Frost was in many ways the epitome of the '60s tycoon. Like most of the new millionaires of the 1960s, he came from the lower middle class. He was born in April 1939, the son of a Methodist couple of modest means. After doing well at grammar school he won a place at Cambridge University. His academic career was undistinguished, and in summer 1961 he graduated with a second-class degree. However, while at Cambridge he also appeared as a stand-up comic with the Footlights Club; a theatrical agent who spotted him said later that Frost's jokes were not very good, 'but this young man carried his own atmosphere'. He was signed up by the Noel Gay agency in London, and at the same time he was taken on by one of the commercial television companies, Rediffusion, as a trainee. After working behind the scenes for a few months he was allowed to appear in front of the cameras, as presenter of a programme called *Let's Twist*. Meanwhile, the Noel Gay agency booked Frost a cabaret engagement at the Blue Angel nightclub, where he was noticed by Ned Sherrin, a BBC producer who was looking for someone to present the new satire show he was planning. 'Looks promising' was Sherrin's verdict. When the original candidate dropped out, Frost was given the job.

The show, *That Was The Week That Was*, went on the air in November 1962. It was a great success: up to twelve million people a week tuned in to watch the mixture of songs, monologues and satirical sketches. As master of ceremonies, Frost naturally attracted most attention. His success also improved his bank balance, as the BBC trebled his pay to £150 a week.

After the show was taken off during the general election of 1964, Frost reappeared as linkman on its successor, *Not So Much a Programme, More a Way of Life*. He also accepted an offer to join the cast of the American version of *That Was The Week That Was*. By 1965, at the age of twenty-six, Frost was earning £40,000 a year. In 1966, following the demise of *Not So Much . . .*, he began two new series: *The Frost Report* consisted of sketches written and performed by other people, while *The Frost Programme* was the first British equivalent to an American chat show. He also founded his first company, David Paradine Productions, which bought the exclusive rights to a number of performers, including Ronnie Barker, Ronnie Corbett and Marty Feldman.

Frost was by no means the first person to see that there was money to be made from television. However, previous TV tycoons had been businessmen; Frost was the first to realise that performers could also take a share of the loot.

Crime pays: When the Great Train Robbers held up the London-to-Glasgow mail train they became folk heroes, 'for they are jolly good felons'. Leatherslade Farm, the robbers' hideaway, was opened to the public by its owner at an admission fee of half a crown.

FIRST TWO VISITORS TO LEATHERSLADE FARM, 1963

Money

When commercial television was introduced in 1955, Sir Winston Churchill dismissed it as a 'tuppenny Punch and Judy show'. In the early days it seemed that the commercial franchise-holders would be lucky to make even tuppence. Associated Rediffusion lost nearly £3 million in its first two years of broadcasting, and Associated Television, the other main commercial station, also lost heavily. But advertisers became more enthusiastic about the mass audience which could be reached through this new medium. The effects were startling. Associated Rediffusion's net profit in 1958 was £4,889,015; in 1959 it was £7 million and by 1960 it was nearly £8 million. Associated Television also had an annual surplus of over £5 million in the same period, and even the smaller regional companies made a fortune. Lord Thomson, who owned Scottish Television, cheerfully admitted that a stake in commercial television was 'a licence to print money'. The quality of programmes was dire—mindless quiz shows and panel games were the order of the day—but, as long as the money rolled in, the station owners were content. In 1962 the Pilkington Committee accused commercial television of 'abandoning the purposes of broadcasting', but the quiz games and westerns continued to fill the screens.

Although the government seemed unable to do anything about the standard of programmes, it did come to accept that the television companies' profits were scandalous. In 1964, shortly before leaving office, the Tory government introduced a levy on the commercial channels' advertising revenue. The franchise-holders complained loudly that they would be bankrupted. The levy was hardly punitive: it did not apply at all to the first £1.5 million of advertising revenue, and the next £6 million was taxed at the modest rate of 25 per cent. The only consequence was that commercial television companies made big profits instead of colossal profits. The continuing financial attractions of the business were demonstrated in December 1966, when the Independent Television Authority invited new applications for the commercial franchises: there was a stampede of applicants, all eager for their licence to print money. And at the head of the queue was 28-year-old David Frost.

Never a man to set his sights low, Frost assembled a consortium to apply for the London franchise, the richest of them all. He brought together a number of people with broadcasting experience, including Michael Peacock and Humphrey Burton from the BBC and Aidan Crawley, a Tory MP who had worked in television for some years. Financial backing was provided by merchant bankers and businessmen such as David Montagu and Arnold Weinstock. Frost's personal stake in the company was £75,000.

In its application, Frost's group promised considerable changes to the dreary menu hitherto offered by commercial TV; there were to be several series on science, more cultural programmes, drama, education, children's shows and original comedy. In June 1967 the ITA announced that Frost's company, now called London Weekend Television, had been successful in its bid. 'Frost Joins Tycoons In ITV Shake-Up' was the *Daily Mirror*'s headline. With the award of the franchise, his £75,000 share became worth anything up to £500,000.

During the year that London Weekend spent preparing to go on the air, Frost involved himself in other ventures as well. He set up David Paradine Films (Paradine is Frost's middle name), whose first production was *The Rise and Rise of Michael Rimmer*, written by John Cleese and Graham Chapman. He was hired by an American television company, at a fee of $40,000 a programme, to interview the possible contenders in the 1968 presidential election. A few months after London Weekend began broadcasting he became even richer by signing a five-year contract to present shows on US television, at a salary of more than half a million dollars.

While Frost enjoyed his transatlantic successes, his television company at home was not doing so well. Its programmes were not

Sharing the loot: Lord Thomson considered that 'a stake in commercial television is a licence to print money'. He was proved right, and in the 1960s owners of commercial stations and the people who appeared on the screen shared the apparently unending jackpot.

Page 137

greatly different from those of the previous franchise-holder, and it was widely criticised for breaking its promises. It also suffered from a strike by technicians, a drop in advertising and, most seriously of all, a hefty increase in the government's advertising levy. London Weekend's managing director, Michael Peacock, was sacked.

Executives of the commercial channels lobbied for a reduction in the advertising levy. Instead of retorting that they ought to improve their programmes, the government obliged, cutting it by £6 million in March 1970. As one disgruntled MP complained in the House of Commons, 'the minister said he was merely relieving them of an imposition, but it was a hand-out to the most prosperous, most influential and least deserving lobby in the country'. The television companies were not satisfied either, arguing that the levy was still too high. In 1971 the new Conservative government reduced it by a further £10 million, and the commercial stations were delighted to find that they could print money again.

Frost, too, had good reason to feel cheerful. He had his stake in London Weekend; he was paid well for his appearances on British TV; and his even larger fees from American television were enhanced by a clever tax avoidance scheme set up in collaboration with a firm called the Trust Corporation of Bahamas Ltd. On 8 February 1969 the Pembina Investment Co. Ltd, a 'shell' company held by the Trust Corporation, changed its name to Leander Productions Ltd. On 17 February an indenture of partnership was entered into between Frost and Leander. The partnership's 'business' was to be carried out under the name of Leander Enterprises, and the agreement provided that 99 per cent of the partnership's capital assets should belong to Frost and 1 per cent to the company, and that Frost should be entitled to 95 per cent of the annual

Frost over the world: David Frost 'rose without trace', and by the end of the decade his nasal intonations had conquered Britain and America. When he invited people to breakfast — including the prime minister — they accepted eagerly; only Paul McCartney declined the invitation.

'profits' of the partnership. These 'profits'—and income—were in fact Frost's American earnings.

In March 1969 Leander Enterprises entered into a contract with an even more exotic company based in Curaçao, which acquired 'sole and exclusive benefit' of the exploitation of Leander Enterprises' assets; and after that date money from Frost's American activities was channelled through these two companies. The upshot of all this was that Frost's British tax bill on his American earnings was £27,805 rather than the £174,654 which it would otherwise have been. And it was all perfectly legal.

By the beginning of the 1970s Frost was the owner of a sizeable business empire. In Britain, he was chairman of Paradine Limited, David Paradine Productions, David Paradine Films, David Paradine Plays and Glebe Music Company. His firms in America included David Paradine Productions Inc., David Paradine Records Inc., Beccles Music Company, Bungay Music Company and the David Frost Show Inc. By the 1980s his future looked even rosier, as his consortium was awarded the franchise for breakfast television in Britain.

Malcolm Muggeridge once suggested that Frost's 'very lack of talent makes him king of the telly'. Certainly Frost was in some

ways representative of the medium in which he worked. Frost in particular and television in general both seemed at times to earn money by sheer momentum, rather than by any definable talent. But the phenomenon was not unique to television. Jim Slater used to say of Slater Walker that 'we are money makers, not thing makers'. At a time when, in some circles, money was the only standard used for measuring success, a medium-sized sum could often be transformed into a huge one by mere inevitability, as long as the aura of success could be sustained. As the *Sunday Times* wrote in 1972: 'The whole circus has become a machine that earns a lot of its profit by generating the premiums that boost its own apparent assets—a seething pyramid of escalating paper.' The comment referred to Slater Walker but, *mutatis mutandis*, could equally well apply to any number of generators of 'fast money' in the 1960s.

The success of Jim Slater was as rapid, and in some respects just as mystifying, as that of David Frost. Like Frost, Slater was a grammar-school boy who at an early age impressed senior executives with his ambition and enthusiasm. He trained as a chartered accountant and then, at the age of twenty-four, was appointed chief accountant and company secretary of a small metal company called Renu Plating, which was part of the Dohm Group. Within three months the owner, a Dane named Svend Dohm, had fallen out with the board of Renu; he promoted Slater to the position of general manager. A few months later, according to Slater's account, 'Dohm made me manager of two of his other subsidiaries, and gradually I went through his group as a sort of trouble-shooter.' Slater decided that the Dohm Group was too small to hold him and in 1955, at the age of twenty-six, he successfully applied for the job of company secretary at Park Royal Vehicles, which made London buses. Park Royal's managing director, Bill Black, was promoted in 1957 to the managing directorship of the firm's owners, Associated Commercial Vehicles (ACV). He made his young *protegé* commercial director of ACV's largest subsidiary. In 1961 Slater was featured in an *Evening News* series on 'The Under Forties'—young businessmen who were expected to go far. When ACV merged with its main rival, Leyland, the following year, Slater went further: he was appointed commercial manager of the whole Leyland Group.

Despite this remarkably quick progress, Slater was dissatisfied. He knew that he would not reach the top position in Leyland for many years since Donald Stokes, the group's managing director, was still a young man. Slater had been dabbling in the Stock Exchange, with some success, since 1960; and he had begun to act as investment adviser to his colleagues at Leyland and, in due course, to stockbrokers. By 1963, in addition to his £10,000 salary from Leyland, he was earning about another £9,000 from his investment activities. He had also started writing a regular column in the *Sunday Telegraph*, under the pseudonym 'Capitalist', in which he tipped shares which he thought were likely to rise in value. These prophecies were often self-fulfilling: following a recommendation by the *Sunday Telegraph*, a share was almost certain to go up, as dealers moved in hoping to make a fast buck.

In 1964 Slater left Leyland to set up in business on his own. Some years later he explained his departure in words that exemplify his distinction between people who make things and people who make money:

> I found that when Donald Stokes said to me: 'I'd like you to go to Finland, we are having trouble with our distributor there. Would you get on a plane and go tomorrow?' I'd think to myself: 'Now, I've got an open position in these eight shares, and the results of two of them are coming out in a few days' time.' It was becoming very difficult for me to leave the country, which meant that I could not do justice to my job.

Jim Slater: 'It is important to realise that in the 1960s British industry was relatively inefficient, and I think that it is now very much better. I think that Slater Walker played its part in this reformation and ... we have certainly contributed to the country's welfare.'

Faced with a choice between productive industry and juggling with pieces of paper on the Stock Exchange, he chose the latter. Within three months of leaving Leyland he had teamed up with another young businessman, Peter Walker, and bought control of a small property firm, H. Lotery. It was renamed Slater Walker.

Reporting this development at the time, the *Evening Standard* noted that Jim Slater and Peter Walker 'intend to increase the emphasis on the investment side of the company's business'. It was something of an understatement. When H. Lotery became Slater Walker in 1964, bought largely with money borrowed from merchant banks, it was valued at £1.5 million: this was the worth of the company's only asset, an office block in the City. By the end of 1969 the company's stock market value was £135 million—an increase of just under 9,000 per cent.

A couple of months after the creation of Slater Walker, Jim Slater made it clear that his policy would be to buy a big enough stake in certain companies to enable him to influence their management; he would then force them to become more profitable 'either by the elimination of unprofitable aspects or by applying resources more efficiently'. There was a certain ambiguity about this. What would 'applying resources more efficiently' mean in practice? Years later, in a interview with the *Observer* in 1973, Slater put the best possible construction on it:

It is important to realise that in the 1960s British industry was relatively inefficient, and I think that it is now very much better. I think that Slater Walker played its part in this reformation and to this extent we have certainly contributed to the country's welfare, as well as in the more direct material sense.

It is true that British industry suffered from dozy management in the 1960s, and Slater Walker's activities may have helped to wake some of them from their slumbers. But a more serious problem—which became even worse in the 1970s—was a lack of long-term investment which would allow companies to expand by purchasing new machinery, hiring new staff and so forth. The rise of Slater Walker did nothing to remedy this, as should have been apparent from the outset. A month after the formation of his company, Jim Slater told the *Evening Standard*: 'I'm just not interested in long-term investments.' The *Standard* report added that Slater 'admits that it is short-term capital gains—outside the six months tax period—that he is after'.

These short-term gains were acquired by 'asset stripping'. The technique was simple, and depended for its success on just two things: the willingness of investors to lend the asset stripper large sums of money, and the existence of companies whose stock-market valuation was lower than their real value. Both these conditions were fulfilled for Slater in the 1960s. He had little difficulty raising money: with his reputation as a whiz-kid from Leyland and his record as 'Capitalist' (in his final *Sunday Telegraph* column, in February 1965, he revealed his true identity), plenty of speculators were prepared to put money into Slater Walker shares. Nor was there any shortage of firms ripe for Slater's 'efficiency' treatment. To calculate a company's stock-market value, one multiplies the price of its shares by the number of shares issued. To ascertain its true value, however, one tots up the actual worth of the company's assets (particularly land and buildings, or any subsidiary companies) and its profitability. By this reckoning, the stock market of the 1960s contained many companies which were under-valued. To the small investor, buying a few hundred shares, such facts might not be especially significant; but to the asset stripper they mean instant money.

Once the asset stripper has picked his target company, he moves in. (The word 'he' is used only because there were no female asset strippers.) After buying control he sells off some of the assets and uses the profits to pay for his next operation. Slater's first *coup* of this sort occurred when he bought a small paint company for about £300,000 in July 1965; within two months the assets had been sold at a profit of about £90,000.

This was the crude form of asset stripping, but the technique was soon refined. The asset stripper would buy shares in his target company—call it Dode Ltd—until he was in a position to make a takeover bid. Instead of putting up cash, however, he would offer the Dode shareholders shares in his own firm. At the same time he would inform Dode shareholders that their company needed more 'dynamic' and 'efficient' management, which he would undertake to provide. This, he said, would increase Dode's profits and, consequently, raise the value of Dode's shares. Suitably impressed, the Dode shareholders would accept the offer. The advantage of this to the asset stripper was, of course, that he was able to gain control of the company without paying real money; instead, he simply had to hand out a few share certificates.

Although few of Slater Walker's takeovers were as simple or trouble-free as this, it was the basic method used during the company's boom years of the late 1960s. Slater was skilled in the art of public relations, and each new takeover was greeted with further praise from the financial press. This praise caused Slater Walker shares to rise still higher, which in turn made those shares an even more attractive 'currency' to offer to shareholders of other companies which were to be taken over. Slater Walker's success thus became self-propelling, fuelled as much by its *image* of wealth as by its realities. The *Sunday Times* was, therefore, not exaggerating when it said that by the early '70s Slater Walker had become 'a seething pyramid of escalating paper'. People who converted those pieces of paper into cash by selling their shares, as Peter Walker did in 1970, made large sums of money. But anyone who hung on, in the fond belief that Slater Walker actually was reinvigorating British industry, would have been better advised to heed the example provided by Jim Slater's 1964 statement that he was 'just not interested in long-term investments'. Slater himself failed to follow his own advice: after selling off much of his shareholding in 1970, he started buying heavily again in 1972. But his days were numbered. In 1975 the authorities in Hong Kong and Singapore began to investigate Slater Walker's activities on their stock exchanges. Slater tendered his resignation, saying that this would make it easier for the Slater Walker board to 'resolve the outstanding problems' in the Far East. At the time there was no suggestion that Slater Walker itself was in financial straits, but eleven months later an accountants' report showed that the seething pyramid was indeed collapsing: in the previous nine months alone, the Bank of England had spent over £45 million propping it up. The price of Slater Walker shares fell to just eight pence. Jim Slater went on television to announce that he was now 'a minus millionaire'.

The collapse of Slater Walker came at a time when the received wisdom of the previous decade was beginning to change. In the 1960s journalists, financiers and politicians had considered it axiomatic that what was good for Slater Walker was good for business. It was the time of the Labour government's merger boom, when company takeovers were thought to bring 'more efficient deployment' of resources. The Tories also approved: the first two years of Ted Heath's government, between 1970 and 1972, were sometimes described as the years of 'Slater Walker government' which would allow efficient companies to prosper while lame ducks were left to die. Peter Walker was one of the most important members of Heath's cabinet.

Walker's political career meant that he had little to do with the day-to-day running of Slater Walker in the 1960s. Nevertheless, as a non-executive director and leading shareholder he could have exercised some influence if he disapproved of the direction which the company was taking. But there was no need for him to do so: Slater Walker, it was agreed on all sides, was the sort of firm which would give British business a good name.

By 1973, however, the climate was different. Several financial scandals led to growing public hostility towards the City. Even Ted Heath dubbed one company, Lonrho, as 'the unacceptable face of capitalism'. In keeping with the new spirit, the minister for trade and industry, one Peter Walker, said that 'capitalism should not be regarded as the means for a few to get rich without regard to the

Peter Walker: 'For two years Mr Walker was national chairman of the Young Conservatives. At the age of 23 he was the youngest Tory candidate ever to contest an election — at Dartford, in 1955.' He was also in Ted Heath's 'Slater Walker government' of the early 1970s.

needs and hopes of the majority of people'. It was an apt description of the money-makers of the 1960s. Commercial television companies amassed large sums without concerning themselves too much with the quality of their programmes. Financiers put their money into Slater Walker without seriously considering the consequences for British industry. Property developers made fortunes without worrying about the effects of their activities on British towns and cities. Fast money seemed to be sufficient justification for almost any kind of behaviour.

The amount of protest directed at the entrepreneurs of the 1960s varied according to the visibility of their enterprises. Slater Walker's growth took place in the secluded world of the Stock Exchange, and was conducted largely by the exchange of pieces of paper. Most people's knowledge of Slater Walker depended on what they read in the papers—and, until the early 1970s, the press was almost unanimous in its praise. But other businessmen, notably property speculators, were less able to hide the consequences of their work from the public gaze. When the *Sunday Times* complained in 1964 that 'there are people today amassing stupendous fortunes by systematically destroying our historic cities', it was only confirming what people could already see for themselves. The traditional skyline of urban Britain had altered beyond recognition.

One building in particular, Centre Point in London, became a focus for protest. This was partly because of its size and position: it was a 385 feet high office block which towered over central London. At the time of its construction in the mid-'60s it was the second tallest building in London. But there was another reason why Centre Point was an especially appropriate symbol of the property speculator's determination to make money regardless of

the social cost: the skyscraper, once constructed, remained empty. In 1969 a street-theatre group called Agitprop (Agitation and Propaganda) held a demonstration outside Centre Point. As one of their leaflets put it:

This building is a public scandal! Like hundreds of others it has stood empty for two years—while thousands of people in this country are homeless or live in slum conditions. There are 8,000,000 square feet of empty office space in Greater London alone—enough to house *all* of Britain's 10,000 homeless families in one go.

It may seem strange that Harry Hyams, the developer, should put up a building only to leave it unoccupied when it could be earning rent, but in fact his economics were perfectly sound at a time when the level of office rents was rising. One of the protesters outside Centre Point explained:

When this building was completed two years ago, office rents were almost £3 a square foot. If it had been let at that time it would have been worth £11 millions. Now office space is worth £5 a square foot, making the block worth £18 millions.

Going bust: Not all the tycoons of the 1960s managed to keep their balance on the financial tightrope. John Bloom's Rolls Razor washing machine company crashed in July 1964; Bloom was then savaged on television by Bernard Levin, and went into the holiday business.

Bouncing back: Robert Maxwell, millionaire publisher, was one of the most enthusiastic promoters of the 'I'm Backing Britain' campaign. He took full-page newspaper advertisements headed '100 Uncranky Suggestions of ways to help your country — and yourself'.

Harry Hyams always intended the building for a sole tenant, paying a high rent. He could therefore afford to sit back and wait for a few years until a tenant was found who was prepared to pay it, by which time the increased value of the building and the extra rent would more than compensate for the loss of income during the years without tenants—especially as in those days rates were not paid on empty buildings.

By the end of the 1960s Harry Hyams's personal fortune was estimated to be £27 million. According to Oliver Marriott's definitive book, *The Property Boom*, well over a hundred other property developers also became millionaires. No great skill was required, Marriott believes: 'They were men who happened to be in the right business at the right time and, given the profit margins in that business, could hardly fail to make money.'

After the Second World War, realising that much urban reconstruction was bound to take place, the Labour government had introduced a 100 per cent tax on any increased value which a site gained after planning permission was given for development. In 1953 the Conservative government abolished this development charge altogether: henceforth property speculators would be able to keep their profits. A year later the government also dropped the system of building controls, whereby no redevelopment could take place without a licence from the Ministry of Works. For the following ten years speculators indulged in almost unrestricted building and money-making. All the developers had to do was borrow the initial money to pay for the land and the building; and since many of them were estate agents, who presumably had expert knowledge of the property market, there was seldom any difficulty in finding financial backers. Between 1958 and 1962 the share values of property companies on the London Stock Exchange rose from £103 million to £800 million.

In 1964, with many politicians echoing the *Sunday Times*'s complaint about the fortunes which were being amassed from the destruction of Britain's cities, the new Labour government banned any further office developments in London. The speculators' profits were unharmed, however, as this measure restricted the supply of offices without affecting demand, and for the rest of the decade rents climbed steeply.

The dividing line between 'good' developers and 'bad' ones seems to have been a curiously random one. For instance, both Harry Hyams and Nigel Broackes made millions from property development. Hyams became a hate figure, viewed with disapproval even by those who normally approve of entrepreneurs: to many Conservatives he became another 'unacceptable face of capitalism', a man who had gone too far. Broackes, on the other hand, remained a highly respected member of the Establishment, consulted by ministers and invited to serve on public bodies such as the Tote and the Royal Opera House.

Broackes, too, was not averse to exploiting loopholes. The Third Schedule of the Town and Country Planning Act 1947 allowed owners to enlarge their buildings by up to 10 per cent of the original cubic capacity. The purpose of this was merely to enable minor improvements to be made to buildings, but in the late 1950s Broackes realised that it could be used to justify putting up bigger office blocks than would otherwise be permitted. The reason was simple and cunning. Local councils would usually give planning permission for an office block only if the total floor area was no more than three and a half times the area of the site. But the Third

Schedule measured expansion in terms of cubic capacity rather than floor area; so developers could buy an old, spacious office building and convert it into a modern block with lower ceilings and narrower corridors. This would often increase the total floor space to six or seven times the area of the site, thereby flouting planning restrictions, but because of the Third Schedule loophole nothing could be done to stop it. Lord Silkin, the man who had introduced the 1947 Act, said later that 'we did not realise it was capable of being abused. It was sheer ignorance.'

Nigel Broackes, the most successful exploiter of the Third Schedule in the lateFifties and early Sixties, achieved wealth and respectability. Peter Rachman, another property man of the time, had success of a rather different sort: his name entered the language. The *Concise Oxford Dictionary* defines 'Rachmanism' as 'Exploitation of slum tenants by unscrupulous landlords. From P. Rachman, London landlord of early 1960s.' Yet he was probably no worse than many other landlords of the time. Had he not died in November 1962, and had the Profumo scandal not erupted in 1963, it is arguable that he would today be Sir Peter Rachman, patron of the arts and friend of the famous. Certainly while he was alive and rich there were plenty of socially distinguished people who were happy to be associated with him.

Rachman was a Polish Jew whose parents were murdered by the Nazis. He arrived in Britain after the war, and it seems likely that he became a black marketeer. He also became a regular client of prostitutes, one of whom pointed out to him how difficult it was for them to find accommodation from normal letting agencies. So Rachman set up his own agency, which would take flats at about £5 a week and then sub-let them to prostitutes, officially at the same price but in fact for about £15. He also rented out flats to 'respectable' people so that if there were ever complaints about one of his prostitutes he could express bewilderment and point to his many 'decent' tenants.

He was soon buying houses on a mortgage and selling them at a profit shortly afterwards. He also bought houses and flats which were nearing the end of their leases, and were therefore cheap; he let them to the West Indians who were arriving in Britain in the late 1950s and who found that few other agents were prepared to help them.

Rachman spent his money as fast as he earned it, and by the late 1950s he was an established figure on the social scene. He owned a Soho nightclub which was frequented by Princess Margaret and the Duke of Kent. At Bishopstone, his house in Hampstead, he gave weekend parties which were attended by MPs, peers, actresses and singers. He had a brief affair with Christine Keeler and then, during 1961 and 1962, a rather longer one with Mandy Rice-Davies.

In November 1962 Rachman's weak heart finally got the better of him; he died in Edgware General Hospital. When the accountants examined his books, they found that most of his property was so heavily mortgaged as to be worthless. And that might have been the end of Rachman, but for the sex scandals of 1963. When Stephen Ward was being committed for trial on a charge of living off immoral earnings, Mandy Rice-Davies was asked to list her lovers. One of the men she named was Rachman, who had a distinct advantage over the others as far as the press was concerned: he was no longer alive. Dead people cannot sue for libel. In the excitable, scandal-filled atmosphere of 1963 he was a perfect target. The mass-circulation Sunday papers described him as a 'vice king' and printed lurid exposés of his 'empire based on vice and drugs, violence and blackmail, extortion and slum landlordism'. The stories were highly exaggerated. It is true that Rachman employed strong-arm men but there is hardly any evidence that he used them against his tenants. His houses were in bad repair and his rents were high, but this was true of many landlords. His morals may have been dubious but he was not the personification of wickedness which he became in the public imagination. However, he was a useful scapegoat. Harold Wilson said that the 'disease of Rachmanism' could be cured only by the removal of the Tory government. Rachman's former friends in high places, who had been only too willing to enjoy the proceeds of his supposed 'empire of vice', fell silent. He passed into legend as a criminal at the same time as the train robbers were becoming folk heroes.

When Mandy Rice-Davies named Peter Rachman as one of her lovers, she described another of them simply as 'the Indian doctor'. This was Emil Savundra. If she had mentioned him by name, he might have been 'exposed' by the Sunday papers in the same way as Rachman. As it was, he had another three years of high living before anyone thought to inquire into how he had made his money.

Savundra was neither an Indian nor a doctor, though he liked to call himself Dr Savundra. He was a Ceylonese Tamil who showed his entrepreneurial skills at an early age by defrauding the Chinese government out of several hundred thousand pounds: he offered to sell China some oil; they sent him the money but he neglected to send them any oil. This success convinced Savundra that, as Phineas T. Barnum used to say, there's a sucker born every minute. He came to England in search of some more.

Just as the somnolence of many company directors in the 1960s left them unguarded against exploitation by firms such as Slater Walker, so the insurance business was unprotected against an operator as ungentlemanly as Emil Savundra. The industry's rules had been unchanged for decades. To start an insurance company one merely had to 'show' capital of £50,000. The sum could be borrowed from a bank, 'shown' and then returned the next day. An insurance company could thus be founded without any actual money with which to pay claims. The idea that someone might *do* such a dastardly thing had not occurred to the staid old controllers of British insurance, just as Lord Silkin had not imagined that anyone would be unscrupulous enough to take advantage of the Third Schedule of his Town and Country Planning Act. Savundra could hardly believe his luck. As he once said, 'When you English see a loophole in the law, you drive a Mini-Minor through it; I, Savundra, drive a Rolls-Royce.'

The Rolls-Royce in question was his firm Fire, Auto and Marine, which he registered in February 1963. Insurance salesmen were usually offered a 10 per cent commission, but Savundra gave them up to 20 per cent. And the policies were easy to sell, since the premiums were lower than those of the other insurance companies. Within weeks, tens of thousands of motorists had insured their cars with Fire, Auto and Marine, whose company slogan was 'Benefit Through Care'. By 1964 FAM was the fastest-growing insurance firm in Britain, and Savundra was a rich man.

Like many other tycoons of the 1960s, from Peter Rachman to the Kray brothers, Savundra found that wealth, however disreputably acquired, could purchase social standing. Politicians and businessmen accepted invitations to lunch in his boardroom. He entertained lavishly at his home in Hampstead and became friendly with Lord Lucan and other young socialites. He took up the expensive sport of power-boat racing. One day he asked a friend: 'How do I go about getting a knighthood?' If he continued to cultivate the right people, it could only be a matter of time.

However, as with Slater Walker, his business had become a seething pyramid of escalating paper which could not be sustained indefinitely. In the early days he had been content to pocket motorists' premiums, but when the claims began to come in the firm had no money with which to pay. By June 1966 Fire, Auto and Marine had 43,000 unpaid insurance claims in its files. Motorists' anger at Savundra's dilatoriness prompted newspapers and the Board of Trade to investigate. Fire, Auto and Marine crashed with debts of £3 million.

In January 1967 the man who had described himself as 'the great Savundra' signed on at his local labour exchange, complaining about his desertion by his fair-weather friends. 'Last year I got 650 Christmas cards,' he told reporters. 'This year I had two. One from my gardener and one from the man who holds the burglar alarm keys.' He was interviewed on television by David Frost, before an audience largely composed of aggrieved policy-holders; he narrowly escaped a public lynching. Late in 1967 he was charged with

Living in style: With the money he pocketed from customers of his Fire, Auto and Marine insurance company Emil Savundra bought two houses, entertained lavishly and took up power-boat racing. 'In effect, you stole,' said the judge at his trial, sentencing him to eight years.

conspiracy to defraud and the following March, after a long trial at the Old Bailey, he was sentenced to eight years' imprisonment. 'You did not rob and you were not armed,' the judge said, 'but in effect you stole.'

Savundra's activities led to a tightening of the law. The starting sum for insurance companies was raised from £50,000 to £250,000 and the Department of Trade was given greater powers to scrutinise company accounts. But the insurance business remained as precarious as ever, as was shown by the crash of the Vehicle and General company, which covered twice as many motorists as Savundra's Fire, Auto and Marine.

Similarly, the Rachman affair brought about changes in the Rent Act; but the most serious problem which it had revealed—the shortage of rented accommodation—was not confronted. Company law was altered after the collapse of Slater Walker but little was done about a much graver weakness, the failure of British financiers to commit themselves to long-term investment. The years of fast money had left their mark.

Some of the 'new aristocrats' who had become instant tycoons in the 1960s became even wealthier in the 1970s. A report in the *Director* magazine in 1975 disclosed that over a hundred British pop musicians were each earning more than £100,000 a year. This

may even have been an under-estimate, for the *Observer*'s business pages suggested that as many as thirty British rock performers were earning over a million pounds a year each in 1972.

Nevertheless, during the 1970s the new tycoons lost much of their glamour. Too many of them had fallen from grace or had been exposed as tricksters for it still to be credible that money in itself was an indication of merit. The people who survived were those who played down the significance of their money. Those who ostentatiously gloried in their wealth—such as the Kray brothers or Savundra—were either dead or in jail. The comparative affluence of the early 1960s raised expectations of which the new tycoons

Baby you're a rich man: John Lennon believed that a working-class hero was something to be. He also developed the rock star's craving for big cars, and paid £7,000 extra to have his Rolls-Royce redecorated in 'gipsy' colours. He later went into real estate in New York.

were the embodiment. When those expectations were dashed, with the arrival of double-figure inflation and high unemployment, the glitter of the new aristocrats began to seem a little tarnished.

WORK &PLAY

'Tube-Work-Dinner-Work-Tube-Armchair-TV-Sleep-Work. How much more can you take?' London graffito, 1968.

In the 1960s British workers had more 'free time' than ever before. Yet the decade witnessed an enormous growth in the popularity of items such as instant food, or sports such as one-day cricket, which used up *less* free time than before.

Similarly, during the 1960s many workers moved from manufacturing industry to service industries, such as catering. Yet throughout the decade there was actually a lessening of service, as shops, garages and cafés adopted the idea of 'self service'. (One self-service garage cheekily advertised itself with the slogan 'service you can trust'.)

On the surface, these developments seem contradictory and paradoxical. A more detailed examination may explain how they occurred.

As we have seen in an earlier chapter, Harold Wilson celebrated the arrival of the 1960s by promising a 'scientific and technological revolution releasing energy on an enormous scale'. This theme was taken up later in the decade by his minister of technology, Anthony Wedgwood Benn, who gave frequent lectures about the urgent need to make British industry more dynamic and scientific. In 1968, for example, Benn declared that 'the public is still stuck with a communications system that has hardly changed since the stone age'.

In Benn's view technology was synonymous with efficiency, which in turn was synonymous with size. Thus the main effect of the 'technological revolution' was a spate of company mergers, conducted under the auspices of the Industrial Reorganisation Corporation, which created fewer and bigger conglomerates. General Electric (GEC) took over Associated Electrical Industries and then merged with English Electric. Two of Britain's largest motor companies merged to form British Leyland.

However, the birth of these giants did not lead to the computerised efficiency that Wilson had promised back in 1960. Traditional manufacturing industries in Britain simply became even more monolithic, and the technological changes that were introduced did not 'release energy on an enormous scale'. Instead, they increased the drudgery of work on the production line.

While industries such as steel and cars staggered along, other parts of the economy skipped ahead. The number of people employed in manufacturing industry declined from eleven million in 1960 to nine million in 1976, but in the same period the number of people working in service industries—which include everything from banking to hotels—rose from nine and a half million to twelve million. Moreover, these figures understate the growth of the service sector since there was also a trend towards self-service. Service companies therefore spent more money on new equipment than on hiring staff.

This bore no resemblance to the revolution which Wilson had intended. He had envisaged that automation would be introduced in productive industry, but instead it had been taken up mainly by what one MP called 'the candy-floss sector'. In 1966 the government introduced a Selective Employment Tax on the candy-floss firms; its purpose was, in Wilson's words, 'to get some transfer of workers from service trades to manufacturing'. The tax failed. There was no stampede of workers back to the factories, and in 1973 the Conservative government quietly abolished it.

At the same time as the shift from steel to candy-floss there was

xide Regulators
ted Drink Machine
specification by -
RIAL GASES LIMITED
CAMBRIDGE ROA
D. MIDDLESEX
ICE COLD
WATER
SODA
WHISKY
FULL MEASURE
SELECT FIRST
INSERT 2/6 WHEN GREEN LIGHT IS ON
O NOT REMOVE
UP UNTIL GREEN
LIGHT SHOWS

THE FIRST 'BINGO SPECIAL' TRAIN LEAVES LONDON FOR BRIGHTON, 1962

another trend which Wilson's government found equally alarming: workers were earning more money, but they weren't producing more goods. In 1959 the average weekly wage in Britain was £13. By 1968 it was £23. Allowing for inflation, this represents a 27 per cent rise in real earnings. In the same period, productivity increased by a mere 3 per cent. This encouraged the belief that British people weren't working hard enough, a belief that was confirmed, in the government's view, by the fact that Britain's share of the world export market had halved since the 1950s.

It was in this gloomy atmosphere that, in the first week of 1968, five typists at Colt Heating and Ventilation Ltd of Surbiton, Surrey, announced that they would work an extra half-hour every day free of charge. They wanted to 'back Britain'.

Their gesture had an extraordinary effect. Newspapers, industrialists and politicians applauded the women's decision, saying that if more people took the same selfless attitude to their work Britain might become great again. Edmund Dell, a junior minister at the Department of Economic Affairs, made a fact-finding visit to Surbiton. The Labour Party put out a 'Back Britain With Labour' poster. Pye released a record of Bruce Forsyth singing 'I'm Backing Britain'. The Industrial Society formed a campaign committee. On 7 February 1968, the day that the National Economic Development Council met to discuss the subject, millionaire Robert Maxwell took full-page newspaper advertisements headed '100 Uncranky Suggestions of ways to help your country—and yourself'. One suggestion was that people should start drinking British mead.

The original idea of working longer hours for no extra pay was soon forgotten—one trades unionist had dismissed it as 'stark, staring mad'—and the campaign dissolved into little more than a vehicle for making money out of 'I'm Backing Britain' dishcloths, tee shirts and trays. Two months after their brief appearance in the limelight, the Surbiton typists were interviewed by the *Sunday Times*:

> It was a big terrifying fuss, but people liked it. We got mixed up when asked horrid questions about trades unions. Thanks to all the interviewing and things we just didn't get any typing done. Going to lunch at the House of Commons was lovely, but we saw all those MPs lying around with their legs up. That George Brown, with his flesh-coloured socks!

Despite all the razzmatazz, the campaign's effect on Britain's productivity figures was precisely nil. And wages continued to rise.

While people earned more, the number of hours they worked continued to fall. In the mid-nineteenth century the average working week had been seventy hours, spread over six days. Since then trades unions have constantly campaigned for shorter working weeks. Employers have usually resisted, but at times of full employment, when Labour is in a stronger bargaining position, advances have been made. Working hours were reduced to fifty after the First World War, and after the Second World War they dropped to forty-six. The 1960s saw a further reduction, from about forty-four hours to forty. This did not necessarily mean that everyone had another four hours of leisure time every week; while the official number of working hours diminished, there was a sharp increase in overtime working. Nevertheless, there was a net gain of about two hours a week in free time.

The shortening of the working week was only part of the story. Paid holidays did not exist in the nineteenth century. In the 1930s employers became legally obliged to give their workers at least one week's paid holiday every year, but it was not until the 1960s that holidays lengthened dramatically. In 1961 97 per cent of manual workers were still only entitled to a fortnight; by the 1970s 99 per cent were enjoying at least three weeks' holiday—and half of them had four weeks or more.

Gambling fever: The Betting and Gaming Act of 1960 legalised casinos, bingo and off-course betting on horses and dogs. In the following five years the amount of money spent on gambling in Great Britain quadrupled.

The rise of the service industries in the 1960s was thus inevitable. As people spent more time away from work and had more money in their pockets, companies were bound to seize the opportunity of exploiting this market. The public sector did so too: the Sports Council and the Countryside Commission were both set up in the 1960s, and between the mid-'60s and the mid-'70s government spending on recreation quintupled.

Before we examine the effects of this boom, it may be worth considering the definition of leisure. Prior to the Industrial Revolution few people in Britain consciously divided their time into 'work' and 'play'. Sleeping, eating, drinking, dancing and harvesting were all parts of a seamless whole. As Britain became industrialised, the whole nature of work was altered; and so, consequently, was leisure. The very words used to describe it are suggestive. 'Free time' implies that the rest of one's time is spent in some form of bondage. 'Recreation' suggests rebuilding what has been destroyed by hours of work. Given the character of Victorian industry, it is not surprising that workers came to see their lives in these terms. Children of both sexes were put to work at the age of 10 and stayed there until they died or were unfit to continue: the idea of a retirement age had not been invented. The number of hours worked was fearsome. Apart from Sundays, the only days off in

'SAVE THE POUND' DISPLAY AT TRADE CONFERENCE IN LONDON, 1966

the year were Christmas and Good Friday (although, as the century progressed, some employers allowed their workers six days' unpaid leave in the summer for Wakes Week). It has been calculated that an average worker in the mid-nineteenth century had just twenty minutes a day for recreation.

Since then, of course, the amount of time available for leisure has greatly expanded. But have our attitudes changed too? Have we altered the Victorian notion of a split between work and recreation? Some social scientists think so. They argue that in the 1960s distinctions between the two became increasingly blurred, as each influenced the other. For example, Stanley Parker of the

Backing Britain: 'It was a big terrifying fuss, but people liked it. We got mixed up when asked horrid questions about trade unions. Thanks to all the interviewing and things we just didn't get any typing done.' After a brief fusillade of publicity, the campaign soon collapsed.

Office of Population Censuses and Surveys points out that the game of bingo, which became highly popular during the 1960s, resembles the work of many of those who participate in it: 'It involves concentration and regulated patterns of physical movement, is supervised by someone else, and allows breaks for refreshment.'

There are numerous other examples of the influence of work upon leisure. A study in 1964 noted that camping on public campsites, where all amenities are provided, tends to be favoured by people with routine jobs; while those in more creative work prefer to camp in the 'wilderness', where they can be apart from other holidaymakers and can fend for themselves. A rather different influence of work on leisure in the 1960s was the tendency for companies to try to advance their business by using recreation as a marketing ploy. Thus firms would take potential customers out for a round of golf, or give them a splendid and alcoholic lunch, or invite them to the opera. These practices had existed before, of course, but in the 1960s they became institutionalised. It is hard to know how much effect they had on sales, but they certainly increased the satisfaction—and the waistlines—of many company executives.

The most obvious influence of recreation on work in the 1960s was the rise in the number of people employed in the 'leisure industries'—television, sports, gambling, entertainment, tourism and so on. Stanley Parker suggests that 'those in the leisure industries tend to allow considerable scope for the "role style" or personalised performance; authority and sanctions when rules are broken are likely to be asserted only when the public are not present'. This applies equally to a waitress or a newsreader.

It was not only in the leisure industries that work came to resemble recreation. One new development, begun in the United States but soon imitated in Britain, was 'executive toys'—knick-knacks intended to make the office look more like home. Other aspects of office design became more homely too. Gone were the bare floors and stern furniture which had emphasised the barrier between work and recreation; in their place came house-plants, fitted carpets, pictures and comfortable chairs. In certain professions standards of dress were relaxed; some people who in the 1950s had had one set of clothes for work and another for spare time found that the separation was no longer necessary. The less inhibited style of dressing probably led to a more intimate atmosphere at the workplace. As Herbert Marcuse put it: 'Without ceasing to be an instrument of labour, the body is allowed to exhibit its sexual features in the everyday work world and in work relations.' Certainly the phrase 'office party' acquired ineradicable sexual connotations.

Obviously, the influence of leisure on work and vice versa varied widely according to the type of job pursued. In 1963 Stanley Parker interviewed two hundred men and women, and concluded that attitudes to leisure fell into three categories.

The first—which included successful businessmen, doctors, teachers, social workers and other professionals—had no clear demarcation between work and leisure, seeing each as no more than an extension of the other. People in this category tended to be those who felt that they were 'stretched' by their work.

The second group consisted of those who considered themselves 'damaged' by their work, including miners, oil-rig workers and deep sea fishermen. For them, leisure was in direct opposition to work: 'their work is done chiefly to earn a living, and leisure functions for them as compensation for dangerous and damaging work'. Their leisure was, therefore, often intense; heavy drinking bouts were common.

The third group was made up of people whose jobs were neither fulfilling nor oppressive, such as bank employees. Whereas the first group saw leisure as a method of developing their personality and the second treated it as a means of recuperation, members of this third category were 'as passive and uninvolved in their leisure as they are in their work'.

The technocrats: Anthony Wedgwood Benn, Harold Wilson's postmaster-general, was of the opinion that 'the public is still stuck with a communications system that has hardly changed since the stone age'. Britain needed to be 'efficient' and thoroughly computerised.

HAROLD WILSON, ANTHONY WEDGWOOD BENN AND LORD ATTLEE AT OPENING OF THE POST OFFICE TOWER, 1965

It seems probable that most of the population of Britain falls into this last group. They are not inspired by their job; neither are they violently hostile to it. For them, the gap between work and leisure has been bridged only in the sense that both are stupefyingly dull. What sort of leisure is it anyway? Erich Fromm gave a gloomy description in his book *The Sane Society*:

If a man works without genuine relatedness to what he is doing, if he buys and consumes commodities in an abstractified and alienated way, how can he make use of his leisure time in an active and meaningful way? He always remains the passive and alienated consumer. He 'consumes' ball games, moving pictures, newspapers and magazines, books, lectures, natural scenery, social gatherings. . .

That was written in 1956. Fourteen years later Richard Neville, one of the editors of *Oz*, took up Fromm's point and published what amounted to a manifesto of the counter-culture of the 1960s, *Play Power*. (The graffito at the head of this chapter comes from Neville's book.) 'Play', Neville declared, 'has been abolished—except in children, until we knock it out of them—and in its place there is recreation—human maintenance.' Work and recreation depended on each other: both had to be done away with. Therein, Neville argued, lay the achievement of hippy culture: 'The Under-

Play Power: *In his manifesto against 'work', Richard Neville argued that 'the play element fizzled out of established culture in the 19th century, when work was sanctified'. For hippies, according to Neville's account, every Monday morning was a Saturday night.*

ground has abolished work. There are no Positions Vacant columns in the Underground press. . . No one takes vacations—do children holiday from play?' In the Underground, work was done only for fun. Thus if hippies set up bookshops, film groups, newspapers or restaurants they did so only because they enjoyed it. 'Every Monday morning is a Saturday night,' to use Neville's phrase. Because the motive was fun and freedom, there was no need for contracts, time checks, fixed holidays or strikes. You could work with whoever you liked; you could disappear for days on end if you wished.

Many people who worked in the Underground might consider Neville's account a trifle romanticised: there *were* arguments and personality clashes. Nevertheless, it is undoubtedly true that the hippies did challenge the pattern of work and leisure which had existed for over a hundred years. As Neville said, 'the play element fizzled out of established culture in the nineteenth century, when

Feeding time: While some people were excitedly trying out recipes for cassoulet *and* salade niçoise, *newly learnt from Elizabeth David, others were filling themselves with frozen food, tinned food, dried food and keg beer. Supermarket shelves bulged with 'convenience' products.*

work was sanctified'. There was one exception: 'Media people enjoy their work. Today, media is substitute play. . . That is why the Underground is obsessed with media in all its forms; why most of its enterprises are media enterprises.' The Underground's best media manipulators had been those with the greatest flair for fun. Jerry Rubin had appeared before the House Committee on Un-American Activities wearing a colourful, antique uniform. Eldridge Cleaver had withdrawn from his campaign for president in favour of the yippie candidate, Pigasus, with the comment that 'the pig is mightier than the Cleaver'.

The Underground's reaction against passive consumption was expressed in papers such as *Oz*, which encouraged readers to criticise it. In the legendary School Kids' Issue of *Oz*, three of the four items in the letters column were far from laudatory. Not for them the polite 'may I beg to disagree' found in letters pages on other newspapers. One reader, Steve Francis, complained that *Oz* was full of 'pseudo-intellectual crap' and was failing to fulfil the function of an Underground paper: 'For too long we, the readers, have sat back and had shit shoved into our brains. WE should decide what we want to read, not just accept what is given to us.' A Spanish reader wrote that 'you do a LOT, but you could do more', while another letter, from a schoolteacher, argued that 'as long as *Oz* remains principally a consumer good, I don't see it as being genuinely revolutionary or anti-establishment. . . If *Oz* was real, it would attract pieces from kids who've lived in Scunthorpe.'

The same desire to change the way in which people 'consumed' leisure was visible in the Arts Lab, Drury Lane, founded by Jim Haines in July 1967. Haines was an inexhaustible young American who had already started the Traverse Theatre in Edinburgh and who found conventional theatre torpid and dull. He believed that the audience should be actively involved in any artistic performance. As Neville says, at the Arts Lab 'it was not unknown for a play to reach its climax at the same time as the audience were reaching theirs, all unconcernedly intertwined with each other'. Often there was no straightforward ending to a 'happening' at the Arts Lab; as the hours wore on and people dozed off, the theatre would become a crash-pad.

The rural communes set up by hippies can also be seen as a denial of traditional ideas of work and leisure. They were a return to work directly related to basic human needs. The people in these communes, by growing their own food, attempted to control what they consumed instead of taking what they were given by the manufacturers of convenience foods. Moreover, they were opposing the tendency for the nuclear family to be considered as the main 'unit of leisure'.

Some of *Play Power*'s ideology lives on in the communally run bookshops and health food shops which are now a common feature of London and other British cities. But there were comparatively few dedicated hippies, while there were several million families whose idea of leisure remained as far removed from 'play' as it had been before Richard Neville issued his cry for freedom. In *Play Power* he had argued that 'the bank manager's ideal family isolates one from another, ill-preparing its offspring for relating to the outside world. Love thy neighbour—so long as he is safely ensconced within his capsule.' Yet the 1960s actually increased that isolation.

In the 1950s many working-class families in slum areas were moved into estates nearer the suburbs, or into new towns. Consequently the slum districts deteriorated still further and the remaining families moved out too, leaving whole areas in danger of becoming a wasteland. Local government planning policy changed direction and the 1960s saw a redevelopment of the original slum sites, with huge estates of tower blocks being built. But this made matters worse. Phil Cohen, a social scientist who studied one of the areas most affected, the East End of London, wrote:

The first effect of the high density, high rise schemes was to destroy the function of the street, the local pub, the corner shop, as articulations of communal space. Instead there was only the privatised space of the family unit, stacked one on top of each other, in total isolation, juxtaposed with the totally public space which surrounded it, and which lacked any of the informal social controls generated by the neighbourhood.

The concept of a 'neighbourhood' had been abolished by a few strokes of the planner's pen; and the system of extended kinship, which had been crucially important to the area's social life, was broken. Cut off from neighbours and relations, the family became dependent on itself. Housebound mothers, in particular, found the new atmosphere claustrophobic; the phenomenon of baby-battering attracted headlines.

Small local industries were unable to survive against their competitors' increased automation and economies of scale. The corner shop disappeared, replaced by a few large supermarkets or shopping centres. In 1956 there were a hundred supermarkets in Britain; by 1967 there were three thousand. The trend towards giantism was particularly noticeable in areas where the local council was controlled by the Labour Party; small shopkeepers were usually Conservatives, whose protests were unheeded by Labour politicians. Two of the most notorious new shopping centres built in the 1960s were at the Elephant and Castle in London and the Bull Ring in Birmingham, both of which were huge, windswept blocks of concrete. As one Tory councillor in Birmingham moaned in 1965, 'The Bull Ring is perfectly all right if one wants an army fortification within the city centre. As a trading area it is a flop.'

An unforeseen problem of these large slab buildings, which afflicted many of the new shopping centres, was the 'rolling eddy'. When the wind hit the wall of a tower block it was pushed down to the ground at a faster speed. It then returned, faster still, against the direction of the natural wind and at about knee level. Some women refused to go to the Croydon Centre, for example, because of the embarrassing effect of the wind on their skirts. Eventually the developers had to put a roof over the whole shopping precinct.

The face of the British high street changed astonishingly fast. As late as the 1950s several parts of London still had shops which sold hay for costermongers' horses. By the mid-'60s these had gone, along with other small shops, swept away by the supermarkets and discount stores whose aim was to sell as many goods as possible as fast as possible. In the 1950s, people usually knew the names of the staff who served in the local shop; by the 1960s, shoppers were expected to serve themselves and take their baskets to a check-out girl, whose face seemed to change from week to week.

The goods bought in these stores were, increasingly, 'convenience' products. Hire purchase was easily available, and people took advantage of it. In 1956, 8 per cent of British households had refrigerators; by 1971 the figure had risen to 69 per cent. By the early 1970s 64 per cent of families also had washing machines. Equally striking was the growing popularity of convenience foods—tinned, frozen or dried—which by 1970 accounted for a quarter of all spending on food. Shops which had previously specialised in selling unprocessed food found themselves forced to adapt or die.

Traditional bakers were particularly badly affected by the boom in instant food. In the 1930s there were over 2,000 independent millers in Britain, supplying small high-street bakery shops with flour; by 1976 only 30 remained. In the 1960s more and more people did all their shopping at the supermarket; those who ran the supermarkets decided that conventional loaves took longer to make than mass-produced white sliced bread; and so the customers' choice was reduced whether they liked it or not. As far as the small bakers were concerned, the most damaging development

High living: In the 1960s local councils vied with each other to see who could build the tallest and most forbidding tower blocks. In the 1970s they started pulling them down and tried to re-create the working-class neighbourhoods which they had so expensively destroyed.

was the invention of the Chorleywood Bread Process in 1962. This was a high-speed method of mixing dough which used a greater proportion of water to flour than traditional processes; it also caused bread to contain more artificial additives and less protein. Only a few nutritionists pointed out at the time that this tendency for food to be more refined, with less natural fibre, might lead to all sorts of diseases from tooth decay to cancer of the bowels. It was not until the 1970s that their views attracted any attention.

Of course people *could* still buy old-fashioned wholemeal loaves in the 1960s but, especially as the small shops closed down, it would have involved a long journey; and, as we have seen, the idea of reducing the amount of time spent on shopping, cooking and eating had become the received wisdom. One of the reasons was that more women were going out to work; they therefore had less time to prepare meals. (A man in the kitchen was still a rare sight.) But behind the philosophy there also lay the belief that time spent on preparing food was time wasted. New industries had arisen to cash in on working people's leisure, and it was important that the number of hours available for that leisure should be maximised.

Much of this spare time was devoted to just one activity—watching television. Most people had already acquired television sets in the 1950s. In 1961 75 per cent of families had one; by 1971 this had risen to over 90 per cent. More remarkable was the number of hours devoted to the set. Between 1964 and 1978 the average time spent viewing rose by 2 hours and 20 minutes a week; for children between the ages of five and fifteen it rose by 6 hours and 18 minutes. Today, the average person in Britain spends about 20 hours every week watching television; and children are the most avid consumers.

This would seem to bear out Richard Neville's argument that even children are having the idea of 'play' beaten out of them. It is hard to imagine a medium more conducive to passivity than television. No effort is required to switch it on; and it does not encourage audience participation or critical reaction. Before the advent of television the most popular working-class entertainments were watching sports matches and going to the cinema. Both these activities require a modicum of energy and will: one has to put on one's coat and travel to the sports ground or cinema. Once television arrived, however, lethargy set in. Why bother to go to a film that would, in a few years' time, be screened in one's own living room? Why go to see Chelsea play Tottenham Hotspur when the highlights would be televised the same evening?

The consequences were dramatic. In 1959 there were 600 million cinema admissions in Britain; by 1970 this had slumped to 225 million. During the same period nearly half of Britain's 3,400 million cinemas were closed. During the 1960 cricket season more than a million people attended county matches; by the end of the decade the equivalent figure was below a hundred thousand. Football attendances fell, too, from 33 million to 25 million.

All these declining pastimes represented what might be called communal leisure rather than family leisure. The trend had been encouraged by the breaking up of working-class neighbourhoods and the introduction of television, both of which made the family more isolated than before. But there was a third significant influence: between 1960 and 1970 the number of car owners in Britain doubled from 5,650,000 to 11,802,000.

The design of motor cars reflects the size of the average British family—two seats in the front for mum and dad, and room for about three children in the back. In the days before most British people had their own transport, leisure travel took the form of charabanc trips or railway journeys; by the 1970s 58 per cent of journeys to social, sporting and cultural activities were conducted by car.

Several companies in the leisure industry sought to take advantage of this increased mobility, the rising affluence and the desire for 'family entertainment'. Chains of steak houses appeared all over Britain serving an unvarying menu of prawn cocktail followed by steak, tomatoes, watercress and 'french fries'. The decor, like the menu, was intended to exude sophistication.

Similarly 'sophisticated' tastes also began to affect that most traditional of working-class establishments, the pub. By the 1960s most pubs in Britain were in the hands of just six large brewing companies. To serve the old cask-conditioned bitters required skill

Jolly japes: 'If a man works without genuine relatedness to what he is doing, if he buys and consumes commodities in an abstractified and alienated way, how can he make use of his leisure time in an active and meaningful way? He always remains the ... alienated consumer.'

and care; the brewers, like the bread industry, discovered that profit margins could be greatly improved by reducing the quality of the product. Whereas real beer continues to ferment until it is served, keg beer is effectively killed at the brewery by being chilled and pasteurised. It is then put into pressurised containers, flat and lifeless, whence it is served by the pressure of carbon dioxide, which makes it fizzy. Its difference from real ale is the same as that between Coca-Cola and wine. By the end of the 1960s, in almost every pub in Britain, the only beer available was keg.

While they were destroying British beer, the brewers also set about changing the character of pubs themselves. Antique fittings were torn out and replaced with a decor not markedly disimilar from that of a steak house—velvet curtains (or, more often, artificial velvet), leatherette chair covers and plush carpets. Plain food gave way to dishes such as scampi-in-the-basket.

The intention of those who ran steak houses and pubs was to offer the newly affluent working class a 'package'—a complete night out, with all the frills. This aim was shared by other sections of the leisure industry, and in particular the travel companies. Package holidays already existed in the form of holiday camps but by the 1960s, with longer holidays and more money, working-class families were prepared to raise their sights. Travel operators introduced cheap package tours to foreign countries, particularly Spain: between 1965 and 1969 alone the number of Britons taking holidays in Spain rose from 803,000 to 1,506,000. Other countries benefited too: in the 1950s about two million British people a year took holidays abroad; by 1971 this total had nearly quadrupled.

Until the creation of package tours, foreign holidays had been almost exclusively the prerogative of the middle class, whose chosen destinations tended to be France and Italy rather than Spain. During the 1950s and 1960s the growing blandness of English food—fish fingers and instant puddings—made some middle-class people think wistfully of the meals they had enjoyed on these foreign sojourns. Their saviour arrived in the person of Elizabeth David, an English woman who had studied at the Sorbonne. Her first book of recipes, *Mediterranean Food*, was published in 1950. *French Country Cooking* followed it in 1951. In 1954, after spending a year researching in Italy, she produced *Italian Food*. But her most influential book was undoubtedly *French Provincial Cooking*, published in 1959. Strange-sounding dishes such as *quiche lorraine*, *boeuf en daube* and *cassoulet* began to appear at British dinner parties. Garlic had fallen out of favour in Britain in the seventeenth century, when it was thought of merely as 'the poor man's physic, of special value to seafaring men because it pacifieth the disposition to vomit'. In the 1960s few middle-class kitchens were complete without it, and vegetables such as avocado pears, aubergines and artichokes became a common sight in greengrocers' shops.

The new interest in foreign food was also reflected in the opening of hundreds of restaurants serving French, Italian, Indian, Chinese, Turkish or Greek dishes. *The Good Food Guide*, founded in the 1950s by Raymond Postgate, enjoyed a large readership among discerning diners.

Eating out became an expensive pastime. Between 1962 and 1978 the retail price index rose by 384 per cent, but in the same period the cost of restaurant meals increased by no less than 573 per cent. Expense account lunchers and wealthier members of the middle class could still afford to eat out regularly, but many of the lower-middle-class people who had begun to visit restaurants found them beyond their means. The number of take-away establishments—particularly kebab houses and Indian and Chinese restaurants—grew to meet the demand for cheap meals, and even fish and chip shops found their fortunes reviving. Noticing the trend, American take-away chains such as McDonald's and Kentucky Fried Chicken moved into Britain during the 1970s. On

GREEN SHIELD
stamps

DOUBLE
GRE
SHIE

TUES

* PUT THE BRAKE ON PRICES!

HEINZ SALAD CREAM	16 OZ	12½p
NESTLES IDEAL MILK	LARGE	8p
ROWNTREES BREAKAWAY		10½p

STAF

- ASSISTANT MA
- CASHIERS
  ADEQUATE TRAINING
  TO SUITABLE APPL
- YOUNG MEN NYS
  A M

POSITIONS CARRY GOOD

WINALOT
LARGE
 15p

STAMPS

ND
LD

SDAY

TESCO
ASSORTED CREAM
BISCUITS

ROBINSONS
SUPER VALUE
DRINKS

14½p

STORK
SOFT MARGARINE

CO

ACANCIES

- **SELF SERVICE SHELF FILLERS**
  & GENERAL STORE ASSISTANTS
  CONGENIAL & INTERESTING WORK
  TRAINING GIVEN

- MALE AND FEMALE
  PROVISION ASSISTANTS

E A CAREER WITH
OPPORTUNITY FOR ADVANCEMENT

NDITIONS HOLIDAYS FREE PROTECTIVE CLOTHING

25p

MEDICATED   MEDICATED

GREENS
MIX
ONLY   1½p

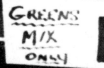

At the office: Out went the bare floors and stern furniture which emphasised the distinction between work and leisure; in came executive toys, house plants, fitted carpets, pictures and low-slung chairs — not to mention sofas. An office was not a workplace but an 'environment'.

the whole they catered for the same kind of people who were the most eager consumers of labour-saving gadgets and instant mashed potatoes. In McDonald's it was possible to eat on the premises; but the plastic decor and bright lighting made it clear that meals were not events to be lingered over. Eating was a physical need which should be satisfied as quickly as possible. The mentality behind this type of consumption was parodied in Woody Allen's film *Everything You Always Wanted to Know About Sex But Were Afraid to Ask* with the invention of the orgasmatron, a machine which provided immediate ecstasy without foreplay.

The desire for instant gratification was not confined to the working-class. In 1964 Terence Conran opened the first branch of his shop Habitat in London. 'We hope,' he said, 'we have taken the foot-slogging out of shopping by assembling a wide selection of unusual and top quality goods under our roof. It has taken us a year to complete this pre-digested shopping programme and we are confident that many women will take to this new style of buying with enthusiasm.' His prediction proved right: the pre-digested shopping programme was a great success because it allowed thousands of middle-class people to buy stylish furniture at a price which didn't rule out short-term use. It also reflected one of the fashions of the age—Conspicuous Thrift.

The idea of Conspicuous Thrift was formulated by Nicholas Tomalin in an article for *Town* magazine in 1963, a year before Conran unleashed it on the shoppers of South Kensington. Tomalin defined the Conspicuous Thrifter as 'a would-be aristocrat, seeking by the appearance of plain living to create the impression of high thinking and anti-vulgarity'. He gave some examples of Conspicuous Thrift in action: 'In your Gothic-windowed bachelor set at Magdalen, you recreate with hi-fi equipment the bleak sublimity of a physics lab. In the Palladian Wiltshire showplace you inherited, you evoke the simplicity of a Scandinavian farm kitchen.' The surroundings didn't have to be luxurious, of course: indeed the true Conspicuous Thrifter would prefer to take a petrol-stained garage and convert it at infinite expense into an 'unpretentious' little mews cottage. The modish CT areas were working-class districts where terraced houses could be bought cheaply and then renovated. When making its predictions for the 1960s *Punch* included the suggestion that the middle classes would move to Islington. It was meant as a joke, but it soon came true. Other parts of London also found themselves colonised by the forces of 'gentrification', including Greenwich in South London and Limehouse in the East End.

Related to Conspicuous Thrift was another fashion, which Nicholas Tomalin failed to notice, known as peasant *chic*. Adherents would take their recipes from Elizabeth David's *French Provincial Cookery*, their clothes from Laura Ashley (simple, printed, cotton skirts), and their cooking utensils and furniture from Habitat. Conran had caught the mood of the market perfectly with his stripped-pine tables and chairs and his plain earthenware pots. Elements of the orient crept in too, particularly in the printed wall-hangings and floor-cushions.

The essence of Conspicuous Thrift was, as Tomalin pointed out, that 'it costs money to conceal the waste of money'. The trend was therefore just as good for business as straightforward Conspicuous Consumption. The *Sunday Times* and Observer began regular sections headed 'Look!' and 'Ego' which often included articles extolling 'delightfully unfussy' floor-mats or other artefacts of the CT age.

The emphasis on simplicity extended out of doors, and was reflected, for example, in the craze for messing about in boats. According to the British Waterways Board, in 1967 there were 6,747 leisure craft on Britain's canals; by 1974 there were 14,557. The number of people who went sailing regularly doubled in the 1960s, while the number of canoeing clubs tripled. Other outdoor

DAVID HICKS IN A PAVILION DESIGNED BY HIM AT NEW HOMES SHOW, 1968

OVERLEAF: THE 'CARRY ON' TEAM ON LOCATION FOR THEIR 24TH FILM

At home: 'The bank manager's ideal family isolates one from another, ill-preparing its offspring for relating to the outside world. Love thy neighbour — so long as he is safely ensconced within his capsule.' The television-watching family was still the main 'unit of leisure'.

recreations such as camping and rambling became more popular too, and by the early 1970s 'activity holidays' such as climbing or pony-trekking were enjoying an unprecedented vogue.

It was the ramblers and the Conspicuous Thrifters, the bargees and the pseudo-peasants, who produced the first organised reaction against some of the changes in lifestyles which had been introduced in the 1960s. In 1973 the *Guardian* started to print a weekly column decrying the destruction of British beer and pubs which had occurred in the preceding decade. In the same year the Campaign for Real Ale (CAMRA) was founded, and by the end of 1974 it had attracted 30,000 members. At first the big brewers resisted the campaign, but eventually they were forced to put back the hand-pumps which had been taken out only a few years before. Watney's, CAMRA's *bête noire*, had spent the late 1960s trying to create a corporate image by painting all its pubs bright red. Several independent brewers set themselves up in business. Ruddle's County Ale—hitherto known only to a handful of beer lovers—was sold in British Rail buffet cars. The author of the *Guardian*'s beer column, Richard Boston, wrote:

> The success of the consumer revolt is important not just to beer drinkers but to everybody who is concerned about the quality of life. If it can be done with beer it can be done with other things.

And it was. Later in the 1970s a similar campaign was conducted in support of real bread. The supermarket chains, like the brewers, replied that they were only giving the public what it wanted; but it was noticeable that they, like the brewers, tentatively reintroduced the wholesome produce which had been banished from their portals a few years earlier.

There were, then, some impressive local successes by those who wished to turn back the march of 'progress'. But they were small achievements. In 1963 Harold Wilson had described computers which 'do their calculations and take their decisions in a period of three millionths of a second', conjuring up visions of a society of leisure, in which traditional attitudes to work and play would disappear. By the late 1970s other politicians were heralding the arrival of the silicon chip in similar terms, and books were published with such titles as *The Leisure Shock* or *The End of Work*. Full employment seemed unlikely to return for many years, if ever, yet governments made little effort to prepare people for this enforced leisure.

A growing number of women had gone out to work during the 1960s; by the late 1970s, with unemployment figures climbing inexorably upwards, they were encouraged to give up their jobs. As one of Mrs Thatcher's ministers, Patrick Jenkin, said in 1979: 'If the Good Lord had intended us all having equal rights to go out to work. . . He really wouldn't have created man and woman.' It was Jenkin's belief that the pressure on women to hold down jobs 'devalues motherhood'. He did not suggest that men ought to share in the responsibilities of motherhood; still less did he give any indication of what women might do during those moments in the day when they were not changing nappies or cooking meals. Apparently, the government's interest was only in matters connected with 'work', whether child-rearing or tool-making.

There were few signs of Richard Neville's dreams about 'play power' becoming a reality, even for the unemployed. Instead of playing frisbee or dancing in the street, most of them said that they wanted a job. They needed the money of course, but in addition to this all their education and training had led them to assume that work was the only way in which a person could gain self-respect.

And what of those who had jobs? For them, too, leisure remained of secondary importance. In the 1980s, as in the 1960s, most of them returned from work in the evening and switched on the television to re-create themselves for the morrow.

Richard Barnes, *Mods!* (Eel Pie, 1979)

Barbara Bernard, *Fashion in the '60s* (Academy Editions, 1978)

Christopher Booker, *The Neophiliacs* (Collins, 1969)

Clive Borrell and Brian Cashinella, *Crime in Britain Today* (Routledge & Kegan Paul, 1975)

Richard Boston, *Beer and Skittles* (Collins, 1976)

Nigel Broackes, *A Growing Concern* (Weidenfeld & Nicolson, 1979)

Eric Butterworth and David Weir (eds.), *The Sociology of Modern Britain* (Fontana, 1976)

Alexander Cockburn and Robin Blackburn (eds.), *Student Power* (Penguin, 1969)

Stanley Cohen, *Folk Devils and Moral Panics: The Creation of the Mods and Rockers* (MacGibbon & Kee, 1972)

Jon Connell and Douglas Sutherland, *Fraud: The Amazing Career of Dr Savundra* (Hodder & Stoughton, 1978)

Anna Coote and Beatrix Campbell, *Sweet Freedom: The Struggle for Women's Liberation* (Picador, 1982)

Richard Crossman, *The Diaries of a Cabinet Minister 1964–70* (Hamish Hamilton/Jonathan Cape, 1975–77)

Richard DiLello, *The Longest Cocktail Party* (Charisma, 1973)

Paul Foot, *The Politics of Harold Wilson* (Penguin, 1968)

Peta Fordham, *The Robbers' Tale* (Hodder & Stoughton, 1965)

George Frankl, *The Failure of the Sexual Revolution* (Stanmore Press, 1974)

Willi Frischauer, *David Frost* (Michael Joseph, 1972)

Jonathan Gathorne-Hardy, *Love, Sex, Marriage and Divorce* (Jonathan Cape, 1981)

Charlie Gillett (ed.), *Rock File* (New English Library, 1972)

John H. Goldthorpe, *Social Mobility and Class Structure in Modern Britain* (Clarendon Press, 1980)

Shirley Green, *Rachman* (Michael Joseph, 1979)

Germaine Greer, *The Female Eunuch* (MacGibbon & Kee, 1970)

Stuart Hall and Tony Jefferson (eds.), *Resistance Through Rituals: Youth Subcultures in Post-war Britain* (Hutchinson, 1976)

A. H. Halsey (ed.), *Trends in British Society Since 1900* (Macmillan, 1972)

Dick Hebdige, *Subculture: The Meaning of Style* (Methuen, 1979)

Gary Herman, *The Who* (Studio Vista, 1971)

Anthony Howard and Richard West, *The Making of the Prime Minister* (Jonathan Cape, 1965)

Derek Humphry and Michael Ward, *Passports and Politics* (Penguin, 1974)

Patrick Hutber, *The Decline and Fall of the Middle Class—and How it Can Fight Back* (Associated Business Programmes, 1976)

Richard Ingrams (ed.), *The Life and Times of Private Eye* (Penguin, 1971)

Peter Kellner and Christopher Hitchens, *Callaghan: The Road to Number Ten* (Cassell, 1976)

John Lahr, *Prick Up Your Ears: The Biography of Joe Orton* (Allen Lane, 1978)

Bernard Levin, *The Pendulum Years: Britain and the Sixties* (Jonathan Cape, 1970)

Lord Longford (ed.), *Pornography* (Coronet, 1972)

Colin MacInnes, *England, Half English* (MacGibbon & Kee, 1961)

Oliver Marriott, *The Property Boom* (Hamish Hamilton, 1967)

Arthur Marwick, *Class: Image and Reality* (Collins, 1980)

Arthur Marwick, *British Society Since 1945* (Pelican, 1982)

Tom Maschler (ed.), *Declaration* (MacGibbon & Kee, 1957)

Juliet Mitchell, *Woman's Estate* (Pelican, 1971)

Mary Morse, *The Unattached* (Pelican, 1965)

F. Musgrove, *Youth and the Social Order* (Routledge & Kegan Paul, 1964)

Richard Neville, *Play Power* (Jonathan Cape, 1970)

Trevor Noble, *Modern Britain: Structure and Change* (Batsford, 1975)

Edward Ornstein and C. Austin Nunn, *The Marketing of Leisure* (Associated Business Press, 1980)

Tony Palmer, *The Trials of Oz* (Blond & Briggs, 1971)

George Paloczi-Horvath, *Youth Up In Arms: A Political and Social World Survey 1955–1970* (Weidenfeld & Nicolson, 1971)

Bridget Pym, *Pressure Groups and the Permissive Society* (David & Charles, 1974)

Timothy Raison (ed.), *Youth in New Society* (Rupert Hart-Davis, 1966)

Charles Raw, *Slater Walker: an Investigation of a Financial Phenomenon* (André Deutsch, 1977)

Mandy Rice-Davies, with Shirley Flack, *Mandy* (Michael Joseph, 1980)

Kenneth Roberts, *Leisure*, 2nd edn (Longman, 1981)

H. Robinson, *A Geography of Tourism* (Macdonald & Evans, 1976)

C. H. Rolph (ed.), *The Trial of Lady Chatterley* (Penguin, 1961)

Lynda Rosen Obst (ed.), *The Sixties* (Rolling Stone Press, 1977)

Anthony Sampson, *Anatomy of Britain* (Hodder & Stoughton, 1962)

Milton Shulman, *The Least Worst Television in the World* (Barrie & Jenkins, 1973)

Tony Stewart (ed.), *Cool Cats: 25 Years of Rock'n'Roll Style* (Eel Pie, 1981)

E. P. Thompson, *Writing by Candlelight* (Merlin Press, 1980)

Nicholas Tomalin, *Nicholas Tomalin Reporting* (André Deutsch, 1975)

Tony Wailey, *Seamen's Strike, Liverpool 1966* (History Workshop Journal, 1978)

Alexander Walker, *Hollywood England: The British Film Industry in the Sixties* (Michael Joseph, 1974)

Aubrey Walter (ed.), *Come Together: The Years of Gay Liberation* (Gay Men's Press, 1980)

Jeffrey Weeks, *Coming Out* (Quartet, 1977)

Jann Wenner, *Lennon Remembers* (Penguin, 1972)

David Widgery, *The Left in Britain 1956–1968* (Penguin, 1976)

Harold Wilson, *The Labour Government 1964–70* (Weidenfeld & Nicolson/Michael Joseph, 1971)